ONE
NATION
UNDER
GOD

D1056944

THE LIFE UNDER GOD SERIES

ONE NATION UNDER GOD

His Rule Over Your Country

TONY EVANS

MOODY PUBLISHERS

CHICAGO

© 2014 by
ANTHONY T. EVANS

All rights reserved. No part of this book may be reproduced in any form without permission in writing from the publisher, except in the case of brief quotations embodied in critical articles or reviews.

Some of the content of this book has been adapted from *The Kingdom Agenda* by Tony Evans ©2013.

All Scripture quotations, unless otherwise indicated, are taken from the New American Standard Bible®, Copyright © 1960, 1962, 1963, 1968, 1971, 1972, 1973, 1975, 1977, 1995 by The Lockman Foundation. Used by permission. (www.Lockman.org)

Scripture quotations marked KJV are taken from the King James Version. Emphasis in Scripture is author's.

Interior design: Erik M. Peterson
Cover design: Smartt Guys design
Cover image: Digital Vision

Library of Congress Cataloging-in-Publication Data

Evans, Tony, 1949-
 One nation under God : pursuing liberty and justice for all / Tony Evans.
    pages cm
 Includes bibliographical references.
 ISBN 978-0-8024-1188-4
1. Christianity and politics--United States. 2. Liberty--Religious aspects--Christianity. 3. Christianity and justice--United States. I. Title.
 BR516.E94 2014
 261.70973--dc23
                              2014007224

We hope you enjoy this book from Moody Publishers. Our goal is to provide high-quality, thought-provoking books and products that connect truth to your real needs and challenges. For more information on other books and products written and produced from a biblical perspective, go to www.moodypublishers.com or write to:

Moody Publishers
820 N. LaSalle Boulevard
Chicago, IL 60610

1 3 5 7 9 10 8 6 4 2

Printed in the United States of America

CONTENTS

INTRODUCTION

You cannot read the Bible and ignore the political realm. The Bible is thick with politics. You have two books, 1 Kings and 2 Kings, that strictly deal with the rule and reign of government leaders. John the Baptist condemned the immoral conduct of Herod Antipas, which led to the prophet's execution (Mark 6:14–29). In Thessalonica, Paul and his companions were charged with committing treason against Rome for insisting "that there is another king, Jesus" (Acts 17:7). And in the greatest act of political and moral rebellion ever against God, the Antichrist will set up his worldwide government of pure evil, and he will rule the earth (Revelation 13:1–10).

Because God is the Sovereign of His universe, it follows that He is intimately concerned with the political affairs of the nations. Psalm 22:28 declares, "The kingdom is the

LORD's and He rules over the nations." There is nothing that happens in the governments of men that does not flow out of the sovereign rule of God. "The king's heart is like channels of water in the hand of the LORD; He turns it wherever He wishes" (Proverbs 21:1).

All through the Bible, we see God placing people strategically in the political realm. He moved Joseph into authority in Egypt (Genesis 41:38–49) and elevated Daniel to a position of great influence in Babylon and later in Persia (Daniel 1:8–21; 2:46–49; 6:1–3). God also placed Nehemiah in the Persian government so he could rebuild his community with government support (Nehemiah 2, 3, 4:15–21, 6:15). He also placed Esther as queen in Persia (see the book of Esther) and Deborah as judge in Israel to accomplish His agenda (Judges 4–5).

In fact, the greatest example of God's involvement in the political affairs of a nation is Israel itself, where God established its constitution, legal structure, and laws that were to be the model for other nations to emulate (Deuteronomy 4:5–7). Along with 1 and 2 Kings, in books such as 1 and 2 Samuel and 1 and 2 Chronicles, God is active on every page: setting up this king, judging that king, and deposing yet another king. There is no escaping God's political activity. This means we cannot divide life down the middle, putting God on one side and politics on the other.

Now someone may argue that while God was intimately involved in the governing of Israel, that was because God

Himself established Israel as a theocracy. But when it comes to the other nations of earth, God is not that deeply involved.

Scripture would not agree with that because in Daniel 4 we see God getting very personally and very intimately involved in the life of King Nebuchadnezzar of Babylon, the greatest secular ruler in the greatest pagan kingdom of the day.

Our look at Nebuchadnezzar begins with his over-enlarged ego that he got from spending too long gazing into his mirror. He declared himself top ruler in the universe, so God sent him a dream.

In the process of interpreting Nebuchadnezzar's dream, Daniel told him God had decreed that Nebuchadnezzar would be rendered insane until he "recognize[d] that the Most High is ruler over the realm of mankind and bestows it on whomever He wishes" (Daniel 4:25).

But then Daniel told Nebuchadnezzar he would get his kingdom back when he thoroughly understood that "it is Heaven that rules" (v. 26). Whenever a government sets itself up as God, it is in for a short run because there is only one King who reigns in power over the universe. God sits in judgment on kings and nations.

The rest of Daniel 4 records the fulfillment of Daniel's interpretation: Nebuchadnezzar was driven from his throne for seven years. I call this a heavenly political protest. God protested the unrighteousness of Nebuchadnezzar's government because Nebuchadnezzar sought to usurp the authority that belongs to God, which is the sin of every centralized government. Nebuchadnezzar wound up making the very confession God decreed he would make (vv. 34–37).

The further a government drifts from God (which means it seeks to become its own god), the more it sets itself up for heavenly political action.

The greatest political statement in the Bible is the declaration of Revelation 19:16 that when Jesus Christ returns to earth to rule, He will come as "KING OF KINGS, AND LORD OF LORDS." Back in Revelation 1:5, John had seen a vision of the glorified Jesus, who was declared to be "the ruler of the kings of the earth."

The Bible also says that "by [Jesus] all things were created . . . whether thrones or dominions or rulers or authorities" (Colossians 1:16). And He not only created heavenly and earthly kingdoms (v. 16), they are dependent on Him to "hold together" (v. 17) and exist by Him and for Him (v. 16).

When Jesus was on earth, He was perceived as a political threat. At one of Jesus' trials, the Jewish council brought Him to Pilate with this accusation: "We found this man misleading our nation and forbidding to pay taxes to Caesar, and saying that He Himself is Christ, a King" (Luke 23:2). The charge that Jesus forbade people to pay taxes was simply untrue, as we will see below in the discussion that includes Mark 12:13–17. Earlier in His ministry, Jesus protested the evil of Herod's reign (Luke 13:31–32).

So to talk about the activity of God the Father and God the Son both in history and in the future is to merge the sacred with the secular in the arena of politics.

After all, in the beginning, God was the government.

Under His governing rule and original blueprint for the structure of limitations and allowances for mankind, there was *maximum freedom*. In fact, freedom was standard protocol. From every tree in the garden, except for one, Adam and Eve had complete and unhindered freedom to partake. This freedom also included the responsibility to manage, develop, and expand the assets God had provided them, the essence of free enterprise.

Yet in the context of this broad-based freedom, God also legislated strictly defined boundaries that came with quick repercussions. If anyone chose to go against the boundaries God had set up, the result would be not only immediate but also dire. While people had the freedom to choose to do wrong, they could not choose to do so without suffering severe and clearly defined consequences.

God's own governing model, then, could be summarized as having broad freedom along with narrow restrictions, followed up with both quick and severe consequences for breaking those restrictions. Yet after the fall of mankind, God transferred the carrying out of the government of mankind to men. He had set the precedent for how His creation should function and then transferred that standard of government to humanity following sin's entry into the world.

Therefore a government patterned off of the original design of the Creator is a government that does not seek to limit humanity's freedoms but rather promotes freedom through the declaration of clear and just boundaries along with the carrying out of immediate and acute consequences for breaking those boundaries. It is in this type of government that individuals, families, churches, and local communities are best equipped to cultivate and maintain high levels of both productivity and enjoyment so that self-government and free enterprise can flourish.

CHAPTER ONE

WHY A NATION NEEDS GOD

All of us are familiar with the story of Humpty-Dumpty, the figure from the children's nursery rhyme whose world was shattered after he had a great fall. He called on the best his world had to offer to address his problem—"all the king's horses and all the king's men." We would say today that Humpty had the White House, Congress, the military, and any other human power or authority you can think of coming to his aid in his brokenness.

But the tragedy of the story is that none of these governmental powers could put Humpty-Dumpty's life and world back together again.

Now it's one thing when a nursery rhyme character cannot find the help he needs to repair his shattered world, even when his problem is being attended to by the highest authorities the culture has to offer. But it's another thing altogether when real people in the real world discover that all the king's horses and all the king's men—human institutions of power and influence—can't fix society's deepest problems and address people's deepest needs.

While the government is never to be looked to in order to solve all of the existing problems, politics and governments were established to, at a minimum, address the needs of those governed. Surely all of the king's horses and all of the king's men ought to maintain an environment conducive to Humpty-Dumpty being put back together again.

But that is difficult to do when the foundational core of national health and stability is precisely what has been broken. Anyone who reads the headlines on a tablet today or who turns on the national news knows that something is slowly destroying America. Some kind of hideous virus, some sort of deadly disease, is racing through our cultural bloodstream.

A SPIRITUAL SICKNESS

When you pass America's problems through the filter of faith and the screen of Scripture, it becomes painfully clear that the problems spring from a common cause, from a spiritual problem deep within society's veins. What we are struggling with as a nation today is very similar to the disease that took the world by storm when it first presented itself on the global scene in the 1960s and then in America in the 1980s, having since claimed over 35 million lives[1]—AIDS.

As you know, AIDS occurs as a result of a breakdown in the body's immune system. As the virus known as HIV attacks and incapacitates the immune system, the body is rendered vulnerable to a host of other diseases. A cold can become pneumonia. An otherwise minor infection can become an aggressive, life-threatening disease. In fact, an AIDS sufferer usually does not die of AIDS itself but of AIDS-related complications due to the body's inability to fight off even the most minor of physical intrusions.

What is true of the AIDS virus is true on every level of our society as well. The core of our spiritual immune system has been badly damaged, with the result that cultural colds have become societal pneumonia, and minor cultural infections have now become life-threatening, to the extent of closing down our government for some time.

Yet none of the medications being used are correcting the problem. At best, they may simply suppress some of the symptoms temporarily. Psychiatric drugs and counseling are not filling our personal sense of emptiness. Workshops, conferences, and even presidential calls for renewed unity are not solving our crime problems. More condoms and sex education are not solving our moral problems. And more activism is not solving our social problems.

Virtually every institution in our culture has been affected, whether that be the instability of the home, reduced educational test scores, a higher crime rate and drug usage, heightened racial tensions, poorer quality in the job market, or an often inadequate and overpriced health care system.

Add to these issues the growing awareness that the government is unable to fix the problems of poverty and social decay, and it quickly becomes apparent that all the king's horses and all the king's men cannot spend enough money or create enough programs to put the Humpty-Dumpty of our nation back together again.

A multitude of books, seminars, workshops, and symposia have not enabled us to fortify our nation's foundational structures. Our technological advances have far outpaced our sense of personal and national responsibility. We can send a robotic probe to examine the surface of Mars, but we cannot manage to pay our bills or wisely choose, as a country, which bills to incur. As a result, our society has declined economically, materially, educationally, morally, and even from the standpoint of our health, all because it has declined spiritually.

Since our national problems and cultural threats are fundamentally spiritual at their core, it is the church that is called on by God to address them. However, despite possessing majority numbers of people professing faith, cultural trends and policies frequently reflect the stronger voice of nonreligious minority groups. One reason for this stems from their unified tenacity in intentionally influencing and utilizing the prominent systems, bodies, and establishments that form our culture.

THE NEED FOR KINGDOM-MINDED LIFE

While the church has done an admirable job of cursing the darkness, we have done a poor job of spreading the light. Thus the church itself has contributed to the spiritual decline of American culture and increase of cultural risks by failing to produce kingdom-minded citizens and entities willing to work together for the greater good.

The tragedy today is not that sinners sin—that's what they're expected to do, since mankind is born in sin and shaped in iniquity (Psalm 51:5; Ephesians 2:1–3). The real tragedy is that the church as a whole has failed to positively transform society and serve as the conscience of the government.

When Christians fail to live out their faith, then their families fail to function as Christian families. Failed Christian families make for ineffective churches. And ineffective churches make no impact on the communities they have been called to serve and change. You can find a church building on nearly every corner in most large cities in America, yet these communities in particular are being systematically destroyed by violence as people languish in poverty and despair. It's obvious that the church is not having the influence that God created and intended it to have.

If we who name the name of Jesus Christ are going to do something for our nation, it must begin with the household of God (1 Peter 4:17). After all, the purpose of the church, in light of the nature of the kingdom, is to develop kingdom-minded citizens and leaders who not only impact the nation from a kingdom perspective but also seek to make legislative decisions based on biblical principles.

The kingdom, simply put, refers to the theocratic operation and implementation of the rule of God over every part of creation. The kingdom agenda is *the visible demonstration of the comprehensive rule of God over every area of life.* The kingdom is not referencing so much a location as it is a source. It is talking about heaven's presence, and operation, in history. Submission to God's kingdom agenda opens up the flow of heaven's involvement in our lives on earth as well as in the life of a nation.

There are four aspects of every kingdom: First, a kingdom must have a king or a ruler. God is the King. Next, a kingdom must also have subjects of the kingdom, the rulers. We are God's subjects. Then, a kingdom also has rules that the ruler oversees. These are biblical principles and truths. And lastly, a kingdom has a realm—a scope over which the king rules. David tells us in the book of Psalms,

> The earth is the LORD's, and all it contains,
> The world, and those who dwell in it. (Psalm 24:1)

The scope of the whole world is God's kingdom.

The rules by which we are to abide in God's kingdom, if we are to receive the blessings and the benefits of the kingdom, are the biblical principles and regulations given to us by the King. God's Word contains everything we need to know and follow in order to enjoy success in our nation.

Yet success has become increasingly elusive to us as a nation because we live in a world where people's first priority isn't aligning their thoughts and actions under biblical principles, but rather they are focused on themselves. We can't solve marriage problems because husbands and wives care more for themselves than they do for each other. We can't solve community crises because many ethnic and special-interest groups care only for their own agendas. We can't solve health and disease epidemics because the bottom line drives pharmaceutical companies to promote more sales rather than promote better health through nutrition and lifestyle choices. We can't put an end to deficit spending because many politicians insist that the cuts take place in somebody else's district.

When we apply a biblical diagnosis to the problems in our nation, the selfishness around us should not surprise us. Paul told Timothy that in the last days, people would be "lovers of pleasure rather than lovers of God" (2 Timothy 3:4). Our world is addicted to pleasure. For many, life is a constant quest for something that gives them that good feeling. And Satan is happy to oblige.

MOVING FROM A ME-FOCUS

As long as we remain *me*-focused we will remain divided, unable to move toward a common goal. When people talk about what's wrong with our nation, the problem they say most often is the government, the media, or the White House—anyone or anything but themselves. The refusal of people to take personal responsibility for their actions has, in and of itself, become a national epidemic.

The root cause of our societal chaos and breakdown is found in this clash of worldviews, those presuppositions that determine how we look at and interpret life.

The worldview of "me-ism," or humanism, puts man at the center of the universe so that he attempts to define man and his relationships solely from naturalistic presuppositions. Theism, on the other hand, puts God in His rightful place at the center of the universe as life's highest Authority by whom everything else must be measured.

Both of these worldviews are religious in nature since both require faith—faith in man or faith in God. Both views also produce a set of principles and standards—an agenda—to be used in determining how life is to be lived. The direction of a society is decided by whichever worldview prevails. It should be obvious, judging by the way our society makes decisions, which worldview prevails. It should be obvious, judging by the direction our society is heading, that we need another agenda—God's kingdom agenda.

WHEN GOD IS ABSENT FROM SOCIETY

I believe that the absence of a cohesive and authentic kingdom agenda, as well as its resulting outcomes, is best captured and summarized in the book of 2 Chronicles, a passage talking about ancient Israel. Chapter 15 reveals why we are failing both spiritually and socially because it reveals three internal elements that plagued Israel, and plague us as well today. I have taken the liberty of substituting America for Israel:

> For many days *America* was without the true God and without a teaching priest and without law. . . . In those times there was no peace to him who went out or to him who came in, for many disturbances afflicted all the inhabitants of *America*. Nation was crushed by nation, and city by city, for God troubled them with every kind of distress. (vv. 3, 5–6)

Scan these few verses, and you will see a picture of great spiritual and social chaos, the breakdown of a society. What went wrong? Three crucial things were missing in Israel's national life, and I believe they are missing today in America as well.

In the situation of the Israelites, the first problem was that they wanted a convenient God, one they could control—a kingdom without a king. It was not that the majority had become atheists or snuffed out their sacrificial fires. Religion continued and rituals remained. It was, rather, that they had resorted to paying homage without alignment, reinforcing the culture's false view of a God who is harmless, distant, and has nothing significant to say about the educational, scientific, entertainment, racial, civic, political, familial, legal, or governing issues of the day.

The issue with a convenient God, one you can control, is that you wind up playing god instead. Any god you can boss around isn't the true God. The true God does not adjust to you. You adjust to Him. The Israelites didn't want the true God messing around in their national life, reminding them that He had an agenda greater than their personal interests and desires. Our culture doesn't want a God like that either.

The world wants a nice little prayer before public meetings, but its people don't want to hear about the true God. And I'm afraid that sometimes the church isn't very interested in the true God anymore either.

The second problem in Israel was a loss of teaching priests. Again, the text doesn't say there were no priests. But the priests had stopped teaching the truth. They had traded enlightenment for entertainment. Worship had degenerated into a social club. The church was no longer the epicenter of all life and conscience of the culture, calling people to take God seriously.

I'm not saying we cannot or should not enjoy worship. There's nothing wrong with celebrating God and expressing our emotions in worship. But emotion is never to replace truth. Israel was suffering from an absence of spiritual leaders who took seriously the authority of Scripture for all of life. Have you ever wondered how we can have all these churches on all these corners with all these preachers and all these choirs and all these deacons and all these ministries—and still have all this mess?

Someone will say, "Well, I didn't like that sermon." Wrong response. The issue is whether it was true, not whether it was popular. Politicians need to be popular. Preachers need to tell the truth.

WHEN TRUTH IS ABSENT

The issue of truth is all-important. Our society is schizophrenic because people want certainty in the important, everyday stuff, but nobody wants to admit that there is such a thing as a reliable body of truth; so relativism rules.

This lack of truth has led to a "conscienceless" society, in which people can sin in large and ongoing ways and yet feel no emotional or spiritual pain. God created pain, whether physical or spiritual, to tell us something is wrong and to keep us from going as far as we wanted to go.

But when people do not have truth, they do not have anything to give them pain when they make wrong decisions. They become "seared in their own conscience as with a branding iron" (1 Timothy 4:2). They become anesthetized, losing their sense of right and wrong. In such a society every person becomes a law unto himself or herself, so chaos rules.

The process starts early these days. It used to be that most people's consciences didn't get anesthetized until college, where the professor in Philosophy 101 was at best an agnostic, or even worse, an atheist. So he would announce, "There are no absolutes."

But now, kids in middle school and high school are learning that one person's answers and ideas are just as good as anyone else's. However, in a world where everybody's answers are right, nobody's answers wind up being right. When a society loses truth, it loses meaning, because people are never really sure about anything.

The third missing ingredient in Israel was God's law.

When a culture has a false view of God built on bad information, God begins to remove the restraint of His law, allowing evil to grow and spread unbridled. Even sinners who respect God's law won't do certain things. But once God's precepts are removed from or marginalized in a culture, then the standard for a society is gone, and the culture faces the consequences of turning against Him.

In Israel's chronicles, God was the cause of their distress, not the sinners in that culture, and not even Satan. It said, "God troubled them." In a situation like that, it doesn't matter who you elect or what programs you initiate. Until God's anger is assuaged, you will not be able to fix what is wrong or spend enough money to buy a way out of the dilemma.

As long as God is kept at a distance, He will not take over the control center of a nation, and unrighteousness will rule. He will be close enough for invocations and benedictions but not part of the decisions in between.

The net result will be the devolution of mankind and the resultant devolution of a nation, as we are currently experiencing. The more we demote God, the worse things will get. This is what Paul referred to when he wrote, "For the wrath of God is revealed from heaven against all ungodliness and unrighteousness of men" (Romans 1:18). What America is witnessing today in the rapid deterioration of our culture is the reality that God is removing more and more of His restraint and revealing more and more of His wrath.

Israel was minus a proper view of God, the teaching of His truth by the priests, and the restraint of His law. No wonder there was great turmoil in the land, as we saw earlier in 2 Chronicles 15:5–6. Let's talk about what was going on as a result. "There was no peace to him who went out or to him who came in, for many disturbances afflicted all the inhabitants" (v. 5). That sounds like a high crime rate. "Nation was crushed by nation, and city by city" (v. 6a). What a picture of conflict on both the local and the international level. Wars and urban conflict marred Israel.

But what I want you to notice is the end of verse 6: "For God troubled them with every kind of distress." In other words, God was behind the chaos in the society. He identified Himself as the responsible party.

Here is a crucial principle we so often miss. When God is your problem, only God is your solution. If God is the One who is offended, you had better address Him.

The root problem is always spiritual, even though the symptoms of it seem social. Israel's problem was God, but there was no one around to say so and to point to God as the answer.

Do I need to say that America's problem is also with God? It is. That's why we'll never see solutions until we appropriately repent and align with God. But it's easier to blame the Devil for our troubles. Verse 6 is surprising because it's not what you would expect to read. You would expect to read, "For Satan troubled them with every kind of distress." When you see disturbances in the land, you would expect somebody to say, "The Devil is messing up America." The Devil is busy, for sure, but he isn't our real problem.

To put it another way, when God is forsaken, unrighteousness dominates. When God is included, righteousness dominates. When God is on the outskirts of all, instead of in the center, we experience His judgment rather than His blessing, and deterioration sets in.

Now here's where the church could be making all the difference if we were really on top of things spiritually. The unregenerate don't know that God is their problem and their only solution, so they go around trying to fix problems using earthly means and earthly wisdom.

But we, the people of God, know that you can't use human, physical, secular means to bring about spiritual solutions. In 2 Corinthians 10:4 Paul writes: "The weapons of our warfare are not of the flesh, but divinely powerful for the destruction of fortresses."

WHAT IS GOD'S APPROACH?

We are supposed to offer a whole different approach, a whole different agenda. We know the first issue that must be addressed is, What is God's approach to solving this problem? We as the people of God are called to bring the presence of God to a society that desperately needs Him. So what are we doing using the same feeble, human approaches to our problems that the world uses?

God has made it unmistakably clear that He must be preeminent. He must be brought downtown in a culture if that culture would be preserved. But when a culture leaves God out, it deteriorates. God will always judge the culture that ignores Him. That's why the Bible says,

> Righteousness exalts a nation,
> But sin is a disgrace to any people. (Proverbs 14:34)

The church has let the world dismiss God. We can't blame the schools for going downhill if righteous parents are never involved there. Their absence means the unrighteous can now dominate. We can't complain that prayer and the Ten Commandments have been removed from schools, when a large number of Christian homes don't acknowledge either on a regular basis at all.

We can't blame the government for deteriorating if the church hasn't spoken up for righteousness in the public arena. We are the ones who take God to the culture. If we sit back and let the unrighteous dominate, they will control our lives. It is our role to bring God to the culture so that righteousness will pervade and God's blessing will be on the culture.

So what are we to do to get us to the point of being one nation under God? Well, let's go back to our text in 2 Chronicles 15 and pick up verse 4: "In their distress they turned to the LORD God of Israel, and they sought Him, and He let them find Him." Israel didn't seek God until they were in distress. God will let you hit bottom, land flat on your back, if that's the only way you will be ready to look up.

Our nation is declining. Our culture is collapsing. But we're still not looking up. And until we do, we'll keep going down. That's where the church comes in. The church must penetrate the culture with the message, "You're going down, but look up. In our distress, let's cry to the Lord. Let's seek Him, and He will let us find Him."

It's not that God is playing hide-and-seek with America. He is wondering how long it will take us to look to Him, how long it will take us to come to Him. He's there, but we can't see Him until we seek Him.

Our nation's pledge describes what we are to be. It says:

I pledge allegiance to the flag of the United States of America and to the Republic for which it stands, *one nation under God . . .*

For some people, this pledge could very well read, *one nation under the Supreme Court*. Or *one nation under me*, or even *one nation under nothing at all*. That, in fact, is our problem.

Politicians often say, "We must change the system." But the last time I checked, what made the system "the system" were the people running it and affected by it, thus contributing back to it. What it comes down to, no matter how many ways we examine it, is that if we are no longer a nation comprised of people seeking to align themselves—and the institutions they belong to—under God, then we have forfeited the blessings, rights, liberty, and privileges that come from being one nation under God.

A nation that refuses to remain under God is a nation that will inevitably go under.

CHAPTER TWO

GOD AND GOVERNMENT

The foundational principle upon which all else should rest concerning how a prosperous, successful nation ought to function is found in Romans 13:1. We read, "Every person is to be in subjection to the governing authorities. *For there is no authority except from God*, and those which exist are established by God."

God is in charge and alone sits as the ultimate government over His creation. All other governments are to reflect His ultimate rule. It is as simple, and as complex, as that.

Scripture states clearly that there is no authority apart from God. Not only that, but we read that any governing authorities put in place have been established by God. Now that doesn't mean that the people filling the positions within the governing authorities are intentionally serving God or that their decisions are in line with God—because many, if not most decisions are not. But the institution of governmental authority has been created, decreed, and established by God, underneath His sovereign control.

For this reason, God cannot be removed from believers' involvement or representation in government because laws are made based on belief systems. Since the Christians' belief system or worldview is to be derived from the Bible, then out of necessity it should inform our politics, and therefore inform the manner in which we both operate and function within our nation.

GOD'S SOVEREIGNTY, HUMANISM, AND MAN-MADE RELIGION

A quick word on sovereignty before we move on, because an accurate understanding of this principle is critical to formulating a believer's worldview on national issues. Sovereignty simply means that God is accountable to no one. He either causes all things to happen or He permits them to happen. To acknowledge His sovereignty means to recognize His jurisdiction, along with the validity of His supremacy, over every area of life.[2]

What humanism often does is offer an insufficient understanding of the sovereign purpose and work of God. These systems attempt to box God into a government confined within the perspective of man. Yet when humanity is used as the starting point for interpreting and interacting with God's creation, faulty theology and sociology emerge as mankind attempts to fashion God into the image of man. As a result, socialism and communism in particular use government to suppress religion to such a degree as to leave the one true God out entirely.

The other extreme of that are those civilizations that, in the name of their religion, create bondage. Many of these ecclesiocracies, and even so-called theocracies, in the Middle East and elsewhere allow people the opportunity to express their faith in the religion that the government has decreed as lawful, but that expression is mandated. That is not freedom. Conversely, that is oppression.

Oppressive religious rule is when government-mandated civil religion is used to rule over people, frequently without the consent of the governed. It includes rule by mandate of an institutional religious hierarchy, and is often resisted by its subjects. In fact, it was partly for that reason that our nation was originally fought for and founded as one nation under God. While the tyranny against which the American revolutionists fought was closely linked to "no taxation without representation," it also included the seeking of a nation with freedom of religion, basing the right of that freedom on the Bible itself. "Resistance to tyranny becomes the Christian and social duty of each individual," wrote John Hancock, the first signer of the Declaration of Independence. He urged the reformers of the day to "continue steadfast, and with a proper sense of your dependence on God, nobly defend those rights which heaven gave, and no man ought to take from us."[3]

True religious freedom never forces obedience, just as God never forces obedience to His rule. As the supreme ruler, He has allowed the freedom to obey or disobey according to mankind's choices within the sovereign lines of His boundaries. The boundary lines of God's sovereignty are the non-negotiable areas He has established. It is similar to the boundary lines in a football game. In between the boundary lines on the football field there is given the freedom to call the plays. Likewise, God has given mankind the freedom to make decisions on the field of life. Of course, disobedient decisions will come with a whistle blown or the resultant consequences, which are oftentimes wrapped into the very activity itself.[4] But in His sovereignty, God has allowed mankind to serve as representatives within His governing systems, for good or for bad.

Keep in mind that God's sovereignty allows Him to even use that which is not cooperating with Him (the bad) in order to move things to where He wants them to go.

Yet while God is able to turn things around, that does not mean that we are to intentionally disregard God's rule. Rather, as the originator of governing authorities and as the sovereign authority over all, what God has to say regarding culture, social order, and government supersedes all else and should be the basis upon which all of our decisions, as followers of Christ, are made. In other words, as a Christian—you cannot discuss government without discussing God. This is because government is a divinely ordained institution.

Problems arise when people adopt the institution of government but dismiss the divine ruler over government. Many people want, "God bless America." They just don't want, "One nation under God." The issue is that you can't have one without the other.

CHOICES AND CONSEQUENCES

God has given us the freedom to choose whether or not we will be one nation under Him—whether we will recognize His rule and operate underneath it. But with that choice comes either "God bless America," or not. God only promises to bless the nation who recognizes His authority.[5]

Freedom means you get to control the choice, but because God is the Sovereign Ruler over His creation, you don't get to control the consequences. He will rule by either endorsing your choice, or He will rule by allowing you to have the consequences of a decision made against Him.

For example, those who favor the legality of abortion-on-demand are making a choice against God's law to take an innocent human being's life. God has given people the freedom to disobey Him in making this choice, even though it is anti-thetical to what He says. And He has even given our government the freedom to issue a law that makes the murder of an unborn child legal.

However, God's viewpoint on the wrongful exercise of this freedom by shedding innocent blood is given to us in Genesis 9:6, where we read:

> Whoever sheds man's blood,
> By man his blood shall be shed,
> For in the image of God
> He made man.

We also read in Proverbs 6:17 that God hates "hands that shed innocent blood." And in Deuteronomy 27:25 (KJV), God curses the one who "taketh reward to slay an innocent person."

When the governing representatives of the people legalizes the shedding of innocent blood (as a for-profit business, nonetheless) then they have placed themselves, and those they represent, in the direct line of God's judgment. An attack on the life of another is an attack on God Himself as humanity has been made in His image.[6]

As a result, there is a price tag for legalizing the shedding of innocent blood. The more that unborn babies are murdered in our land, the more we can expect violence in our culture as well. Because when a culture goes against God's laws, God will allow that culture to experience the consequences of the breaking of that law, in this case the resultant devaluing of life and its effects.

Examining the statistics concerning homicide rates in the United States in correlation with the implementation of legalized abortion in 1973, we see the effects of our nation's official devaluing of life played out amongst ourselves. From 1950–1970, there was an average of 4.2 homicides per 100,000 in the population. Yet in the next three decades (1970–1999), that number more than doubled to an average of nine homicides per 100,000 in the population.[7]

God has made it clear that He will allow the natural consequences of our choices that go against Him. He is the ultimate authority, and everyone else is the delegated authority, for good or for bad. The real issue at hand is how God is going to respond to a culture when the majority of the people seek to veto Him. We can choose our decisions as a nation, but in doing so we are also inviting our consequences.

The Bible tells us that we are all "under God." We read in Psalm 103:19 that, "The LORD has established His throne in the heavens, and His sovereignty rules over all." In Daniel 4, it says that "the Most High is ruler over the realm of mankind" (v. 17) and that "it is Heaven that rules" (v. 26).

Scripture clearly distinguishes for us in these places and in many others that God's rule operates universally over everything, every nation, every person, and every system whether that be political, economic, educational, or familial. Yet while there is one ultimate Ruler, there are multiple rulers who have been put in place in order to rule. That is why Paul tells us to be in subjection to the governing authorities, plural, as we read earlier in Romans 13.

The reason for the plurality in governing authorities is because the division of power provides the best environment for the fair dispersal of power underneath the ultimate ruler, God.

It is in dividing up governing authorities that both checks and balances are put in place against such evils arising within a sinful humanity such as tyranny and dictatorships. That is why our founding fathers separated the judicial from the legislative and also from the executive branches. Since God exists as both unity and diversity (Trinity), human government has been established to reflect that pattern by being unified in their purpose while being diversified in their spheres of responsibility.

The division of power is the biblical and most optimal way for maximizing God's position as the ultimate authority. Government cannot be all things to all people. Only God can be everything for the people. When the state seeks to adopt such a role, it is seeking to emulate God.

THE FOUR SPHERES OF GOVERNMENT

Underneath God's rule, He has broken up the governmental systems into four distinct spheres: Individual, Family, Church, and Civil Government—each having specific limited areas of responsibility and jurisdiction. Since God alone is the ultimate authority, no human government can be.

The first governmental system is also the most important of all four. This is because if this form of government is out of place, then the other three will reflect it. Or if this form of government is functioning properly, the other three will reflect that as well.

FORMS OF GOVERNMENT GIVEN BY GOD

The first and foundational form of government instituted by God is *self-government*.[8] The goal of self-government is to govern oneself according to the principles and precepts found in God's law. When individuals are living life in light of an attitude of self-government, then there is less of a need for anyone or anything else to govern them. In Ecclesiastes 12:13–14, God makes it clear what the fundamental piece of self-government entails and that is the fear of Him. We read,

> The conclusion, when all has been heard, is: fear God and keep His commandments, because this applies to

every person. For God will bring every act to judgment, everything which is hidden, whether it is good or evil.

The next type of government that God prescribes in Scripture is *family government*. God established the family as the foundation of civilization.[9] The Bible tells us that Christ is the head of the husband and the husband is the head of the wife and parents are the head over their children.[10] Scripture goes on to lay out the governing principles in relation to the marriage covenant and family unit. The saga of the nation is the saga of its families written large.

Along with individual and family government, God has also ordained *church government*. The church leaders, as members of the *ecclesia* (the governing body set up by Jesus Christ on His behalf) are to govern matters that apply to the church and/or church members as needed, and serve as the moral conscience of the government. This role is crucial since the progress of a nation is directly related to the state of its morality.[11]

The fourth system of government instituted by God in His kingdom rule on earth is *civil government*. Civil government is that system which has been set in place to maintain a safe, just, and righteous environment in which freedom can flourish. It is a representative system designed to manage society in an orderly fashion. Yet it is to do so without interfering with, negating, or contradicting God's other governing agencies. Civil government is to support, not replace, the other two institutions of government (family and church) so that self-government, and therefore maximum freedom, can be experienced.

Paul emphasizes the primary purpose of civil government in the continuation of his discussion in Romans 13:2–3 when he says,

> Therefore whoever resists authority has opposed the ordinance of God; and they who have opposed will receive condemnation upon themselves. For rulers are not a cause of fear for good behavior, but for evil.

In this verse, Paul introduces us to the one overarching job of civil government which is to promote the conditions for the well-being of the citizenry for good while protecting the citizenry against the proliferation of evil. And since civil government is to operate under God, He—and not man—must be the ultimate standard of what is good, or evil. This means that politics is fundamentally an ethical enterprise based on what is right and what is wrong.

When the government successfully keeps evil in check, good can flourish. This holds true whether that means keeping the evil out that shows up in our enemies around the world, or whether that means keeping people from knocking down your front door. Government is to restrict the flow of evil while simultaneously and intentionally seeking to facilitate conditions to expand the flow of good. Everything within civil government ought to be aimed at this one primary goal.

Paul explains,

> Do you want to have no fear of authority? Do what is good and you will have praise from the same; *for it is a minister of God to you for good.* But if you do what is evil, be afraid; for it does not bear the sword for nothing; for it is a minister of God, *an avenger who brings wrath on the one who practices evil.* (Romans 13:3–4)

When civil government attempts to do more than that, it typically ends up infringing on other divinely authorized governments (individual, family, and/or church). When the government tries to act as someone's parent and pay someone's bills while they do not work, the government has become more than the government was designed to be. The Bible says if a man does not work, he ought not to eat (2 Thessalonians 3:10). It is not talking about when a man cannot work. It is talking about when a man will not work. If a man does not work, you do not offer him a welfare check to pay him for his irresponsibility. You don't look to the government to subsidize laziness and irresponsibility while taxing others to cover the costs.

Just as God restricts the church from giving charity to people prior to getting the family involved first,[12] civil government is not to provide charity prior to the involvement of the family, church, and other local charitable entities. This is so because help is to be given by those closest related to the need, who can provide both love and accountability that promotes personal freedom and responsibility.

What government can do in making this happen is to create an environment for compassion to flourish. That falls underneath its task to promote good. When this order is reversed, then the state becomes an all-encompassing promoter of federal economic dependency leading to illegitimate and irresponsible personal and corporate welfare. Limited government, however, does not mean uncaring and uncompassionate government. Civil government should provide a safety net for those responsible people who fall through the cracks of God's other governmental entities, but such a safety net should always come coupled with accountability that incentivizes them to ultimately get off of it and support themselves.

Such government assistance for able-bodied citizens should be temporary and should not be designed to produce long-term dependency and an entitlement mentality. Government assistance should always be accompanied with accountability for demonstrating responsibility through various means such as developing an employable skill or volunteerism. For example, parents who receive Head Start money for their children's lunch should be required to volunteer at the school that is serving their child.

When civil government is limited to its primary role, while maintaining an environment for God's other governments to flourish, it does not overextend itself and those underneath it by trying to be everything to everybody.

An overextended civil government and overtaxed citizenry limit the freedoms of individuals to pursue their calling under God and their capacity to contribute to economic development. It also creates an environment of restriction, doubt, and concern thus stifling opportunity, ingenuity, and growth.

UNJUST TAXATION

Scripture is clear that everything belongs to God (see Psalm 24:1). So while Jesus' answer with regard to the question on whether a Roman citizen should pay taxes to Caesar *legitimized* human civil government (Mark 12:14–17), it also *limited* human civil government. He said, "Render to Caesar the things that are Caesar's and to God the things that are God's" (v. 17). You only give to civil government that which God has authorized it to be responsible for.

The problem comes when civil government tries to be more than it was designed to be or fails to protect or promote that which government was designed to protect or promote (personal responsibility, family, church, and other private local expressions of charity). When civil government expands and reaches into the other three spheres of government God has instituted (personal, family, and church), tyranny results. We see this reflected in high, illegitimate taxation, subsequently causing civil government to grow far beyond its divinely authorized scope—allowing it to illegitimately confiscate and redistribute that which is not lawfully theirs, as was in the case of 1 Samuel 8:10–18.

The economic responsibility of civil government is to remove fraud and coercion from the marketplace, thus keeping it free from tyranny. It is not to control the marketplace. At best, it should seek to compete in the marketplace, demonstrating its ability to function efficiently, effectively, and for a profit rather than control the marketplace because of its size, power, or ability to print money.

Centralized governmental control of trade is the economic system of the Antichrist.[13] This means that the centralized governmental ownership or control of the ways and means of production is against God (i.e. socialism and communism).

Another hindrance to a stable national economy occurs when a government overtaxes its people. I am talking about democratic governments here too. Whenever the government increasingly taxes your income, it commits a systemic evil. When Israel first demanded a king, Samuel warned the people that if they got a king he would take the best of their produce for his court and impose heavy taxes on them (1 Samuel 8:10–18). High taxation, then, is an indication of divine judgment.

Samuel was saying that the king would demand more of the people than they were obligated to give to God Himself. God required 10 percent, the tithe, as the basic financial obligation for His people.

The king would demand more than that, Samuel told the Israelites. He was saying that no government should demand more from its people than the person who owns it all, who is God. Low taxation of necessity means limited civil government. The only federal income tax in America should be either a flat tax, or a consumption tax.

Whenever civil government taxes its people more than 10 percent of their income, it is committing an injustice. We are under that evil, but it is also partly our fault. We have asked the government to do things that government was never meant to do, and the government is charging us for those services at a much higher rate than would be necessary if we were properly decentralized.

Because Christians have robbed God of His tithe, we are paying much more than that amount (up to 40 percent) in unjust taxation as God's judgment on our spiritual theft.

Once we ask the government to take over things like charity, medical care, and education, government is going to tax us excessively to pay for all of those systems. And when government begins performing illegitimate functions, it becomes spiritually bankrupt—because economics and taxation together form a spiritual issue.

Many of our state governments have come to the conclusion that they cannot be productive enough through legitimate efforts to raise the money they need to operate. So they lay an unofficial tax on their people by setting up a lottery in which luck is substituted for productive work.

So the people, primarily poor people who can't afford it, are enticed to try to luck their way into riches while the state gathers a source of income not tied to productivity.

Of course, the reality is a person has a better chance of finding oil in his backyard than of winning the lottery. Unjust taxation stems from an unbiblical view of life. It's another form of theft.

REPRESENTATIVE GOVERNMENT

The primary intended outcome of a properly functioning civil government promotes a concept we often throw around lightly in our nation today, that of freedom. It is quite possible that our freedoms are often seen with such little value because we have never had to comprehend a life without them, like so many others around the world. We'll look at freedom more closely in the next chapter, but as we conclude this one, let me introduce the concept that civil government exists to promote personal and collective freedom through resisting evil and overseeing the proliferation of good through maintaining a just society. When a government fails to do this, either because it runs inefficiently or ineffectively, it is typically the masses who suffer as a result.

That is why it is essential for the masses, particularly the masses that align themselves underneath Jesus Christ, to live according to the principles and values of the kingdom of God, and to seek to elect representatives who will do the same. Ultimately, this determines how God as Sovereign Ruler will relate to and work through those within and underneath the government and its systems. This is because God relates to us oftentimes based on how His representatives relate to Him.

For example, in the governmental institution of the family a large part of how God relates to, blesses, or does not bless a family has to do with the male leader who has been assigned to cover the family. If the man is not in alignment underneath Jesus Christ and is himself not covered by God's care, protection, and favor—then the family will experience the consequences of this disorder.

In 1 Peter 3:7, we read that a man who does not carry out his role well in relation to God's rule of love in accordance with leading his wife will have his prayers hindered. If his prayers are hindered, then those under his care and covering will not be the recipients of all of the blessing and favor that could be theirs as a result of their leader seeking and being heard by God in prayer on their behalf.

Likewise, how God's representatives in civil government relate to Him frequently affects how He relates collectively to those underneath their leadership as well. Because this is so, it is even more important that you and I as believers elect representatives who best reflect God's rule and God's laws.

CHAPTER THREE

A NATION
AND FREEDOM

I love New York City. If I could pick anywhere in America to go for a week, I would choose New York. The streets are alive with activity and vitality at any time of night or day. One of the things I have always loved most about New York City is its diversity. Walking down the crowded streets, riding in a cab, or stopping in a store or restaurant takes one across the path of people from a variety of cultural backgrounds.

It shouldn't be a surprise that the Big Apple is full of so many different groups of people. After all, there is a lady standing in her harbor whose crown has seven spikes representing the seven seas and seven continents whose inhabitants have been invited to come. Inscribed near a broken chain at the base of Lady Liberty read these words,

Give me your tired, your poor,
Your huddled masses yearning to breathe free,
The wretched refuse of your teeming shore.
Send these, the homeless, tempest-tossed to me:
I lift my lamp beside the golden door.

Lady Liberty proclaims freedom every day to anyone with a heart to hear her. Yet although the opportunity to experience the benefits of legal freedom exists in our nation today, many people still live in bondage to a number of injustices in our nation. These can include economic, relational, societal, educational, health, legal, vocational, or familial injustices.

Despite this reality, our Lady of Liberty still stands for the hope of freedom even though all have not yet found her.

We are going to take a deeper look together at justice and injustice in the following chapter, but first it is important to uncover all of the nuances and possibilities of this term, *freedom*, and how it pertains to us as a nation but also how it pertains to us as individuals, since the bedrock of a society is its individuals.

LET FREEDOM RING

Freedom is something that has been known to many throughout the years both in America and abroad as an elusively tantalizingly gift, a carrot, or a quest.

At the core of American society—at its inception—is located this philosophy, or concept, of freedom. In fact, even though it was forbidden to multitudes through servitude and slavery, freedom was to be the hallmark by which our country and culture should be defined.

Today, we boldly declare, and frequently as well, that we live in both the land of the free and the home of the brave, and in many ways we do. We beckon men and women—families from around the world—to enter into our land, offering them the symbolically broken chains at the base of our Lady. We sing about freedom, write books about freedom, and we make movies about freedom.

Somehow, still to this day, freedom captures our imagination and awakens the deepest core of our spirit within. We can't seem to get enough of this ideological ambition. In the words of Martin Luther King Jr.: "And so let freedom ring from the prodigious hilltops of New Hampshire. Let freedom ring from the mighty mountains of New York."[14] We urge our nation to let freedom ring.

And yet with all of that, and more, there remains a question on the floor that begs for an answer, that seeks a definition. What exactly is this freedom anyhow?

Freedom is the hallmark on which our nation's foundation stands, and yet we have sometimes failed to encapsulate into exact words the complete profundity of its meaning. Freedom from a biblical perspective can be defined as the *release from illegitimate bondage so that you can experience the opportunity to choose to exercise responsibility in maximizing all that you were created to be.*

GOD'S ESTABLISHMENT OF FREEDOM

The first person to use the word *freedom* is God, and He used it in connection with the creation narrative as found in Genesis 2. Freedom is God's gift to mankind. His understanding of this term should be our understanding of this term because His understanding embodies divine truth. Through discovering God's view of freedom, we can also discover what it should mean for us, for our culture, and for society at large.

God told the first man who ever lived, Adam, about freedom. We read,

> Then the LORD God took the man and put him into the garden of Eden to cultivate it and keep it. The LORD God commanded the man, saying, "From any tree of the garden you may eat *freely*; but from the tree of the knowledge of good and evil you shall not eat, for in the day that you eat from it you will surely die. (Genesis 2:15–17)

Here we uncover the very first reference to freedom in the Scriptures. This is important to note due to the biblical hermeneutic called the Law of First Mention. The Law of First Mention simply states that when you want to find the meaning of a term used in Scripture, find the first place that it is used and define its meaning there. Then, be consistent with that meaning throughout the Bible, only changing it if the text itself tells you or allows you to change it at a later point.

The first thing I want to point out, as I noted briefly in the introduction, is that when God created man in the garden, God Himself was the government. God was the sum total of the societal structures, including establishing the dignity of work, the primacy of the family, and the stewardship of His creation. He set the governing rules for how mankind was to function. He instructed man in this first declaration of freedom that from *any* tree of the garden he may freely eat, except for one.

From the start, freedom is a broad concept because the ability to eat from any and every tree except for one is a lot of freedom. If Adam wanted to eat apples, he could eat apples. If he wanted to eat oranges, he could eat oranges. If he wanted pears, he could eat pears. The unrestricted variety and opportunity open to Adam was endless, except for one.

By this we can determine the first thing about God's establishment of freedom which is that it is the maximum opportunity to enjoy and partake in whatever God legitimately provides. At the very heart of freedom is the ability to experience that which God has given, *freely*. If it was legitimately provided by God, you are free to partake of it by your decision or choice. Therefore, according to God's introduction of the term, freedom is very broad.

However, keep in mind that God goes on to stipulate the one tree from which Adam is not to eat—the tree of knowledge of good and evil. Therefore, freedom does not delineate any restrictions at all. God clearly gives a very specific restriction in the midst of telling Adam that he is free. In other words, freedom always comes with boundaries.

Freedom never means the removal of all boundaries, since boundaries are an essential component of actualizing freedom. For example, a tennis player isn't free to play tennis if there is no base line. A baseball player isn't free to play baseball if there is no foul line. A fish is not free to roam the jungle, nor is a lion free to live in the ocean. The reason that God allows boundaries is to create the opportunity to take full advantage of freedom. Without boundaries, chaos inevitably ensues.

As I write this chapter, the football season is in full force. Every week, spectators from around the city head to their favorite venue to either huddle together in the snowfall or enjoy the brisk sun of a game held in one of our warmer parts of the land. Large amounts of money—even larger depending on which team you live near—is paid to afford people the opportunity to spend three, sometimes four, hours watching twenty-two men battle head-to-head, arm-to-arm, and shoulder-to-shoulder. In this game, passion, force, and power join with precision and skill as two teams face off in an epic display of both might and will.

Yet none of that gladiator-style battle could take place without legitimate restrictions of boundaries. No one, not even the players, can enjoy a football game unless there are sidelines and goal lines. Suppose the running back decided that he didn't feel up to being tackled that day, so he chose to avoid the whole fiasco by running into the stands, out into the walkway, past the nachos, hot dogs, and overpriced sodas, and then back down onto the field at the opposing team's goal line.

As he stood there to start his end zone celebration, there is no doubt that an eruption of protests would overtake the players and coaches on the field as well as the fans in the bleachers simply because this running back had violated the laws of freedom. I'm fairly certain he would be suspended, if not entirely removed from the NFL—and then later checked into a mental health facility. Such a blatant disrespect for legitimate boundaries would have ruined the entire experience of the thousands—or nearly a hundred thousand if you are from Dallas like me—who had come to watch the game.

It is difficult to imagine that one man could negatively impact such a large number of people. But he can, just as Adam impacted the entire human race when he broke the one restriction of his freedom by eating from the tree. "Therefore, just as through *one man* sin entered into the world, and death through sin, and so death spread to all men" (Romans 5:12a). The violation of legitimate, authorized boundaries destroys freedom.

When you seek to take advantage of freedom by erasing the legitimate boundaries that the divine Designer has put in place, you wind up with a life coupled with the experience of death . . . death in your dreams, relationships, health, stability, the social order, and more. Because while you are still allowed the opportunity within freedom to choose what you do, what you don't get to choose are the consequences attached to your choice. These consequences are imposed, or allowed, from God, since He is the Ruler of His creation. When society refuses to submit to God, it winds up submitting to chaos (see 2 Chronicles 15:3–6).

In Adam's case he was told, "For in the day that you eat from it *you will surely die*" (Genesis 2:17). The penalty found within God's establishment of freedom was both maximum and immediate. The day that Adam and Eve ate from the restricted tree, they experienced a spiritual death and a removal from the garden that has remained with humanity since that time.

God's kingdom is run by God's rules, and when those rules are broken by individuals or governments, God enacts a consequence to the choice that was made.

Having looked at the consequences of breaking God's restrictions in the midst of freedom, I want to point out something important about those restrictions. While there was maximum freedom to enjoy, there was also only minimal restriction attached. There was only one tree from which Adam and Eve couldn't partake. Essentially, their freedom to do what they wanted to do was much larger than their limitations within that freedom. Keep in mind that biblical freedom is the ability to enjoy and experience the maximum legitimate provisions of God. God didn't place unnecessary restrictions on Adam and Eve in the garden. He didn't handcuff them with a legalistic list of things to do and not to do.

In fact, the New Testament reemphasizes this point of maximum enjoyment with minimal restrictions in Paul's letter to Timothy where we read, "Instruct those who are rich in this present world not to be conceited or to fix their hope on the uncertainty of riches, but on God, *who richly supplies us with all things to enjoy*" (1 Timothy 6:17). Paul did not condemn the wealthy for having wealth; rather he sought to give them wisdom on how best to enjoy that which God Himself had supplied, through imparting a spiritual perspective to the tangible blessings God had given.

Therefore, in summary, God's establishment of freedom included broad opportunities coupled with minimal restrictions followed up with swift and severe consequences for breaking the restrictions. This then should be the paradigm for every society's understanding and implementation of freedom.

BOUNDARIES IN FREEDOM

We are living in a nation today that tends to disregard God's boundaries, insist on full freedom, and complain if any consequences arise as a result. Yet what we must understand in God's kingdom agenda is that if we replace God's establishing criteria of freedom with our own manmade desires for freedom, then all those who abide by our man-made desires will suffer as a result. The cultural chaos that we are experiencing today is intimately tied to the failure of society to abide by God's prescribed boundaries within the freedom that He offers.

God's boundaries exist for a number of reasons: to give us protection, to give us structure, and also to remind us that He is in charge. God placed the tree that Adam and Eve could not eat from directly in the middle of the garden. He didn't hide it somewhere that they would rarely come across it. He positioned it directly in front of their eyes. This was so that the tree would serve as a perpetual reminder that they do not call the shots in the garden.

It was an ongoing symbol to cause humanity to remember that they were under the authority of Someone else. The tree stood stationed strongly to reflect that the government of the garden was God Himself. And since the government was God, then Adam and Eve were not the ones to determine what would be considered good and what would be considered evil within it. That was outside of their jurisdiction as the creature and not the Creator.

To put it another way, the tree of the knowledge of good and evil was a statement to both Adam and Eve that they were to get their information by revelation rather than by reason. They were to receive instruction from God on what was right and what was wrong rather than reason their own ways to their own conclusions. Knowledge was never to come independently of God's perspective on it because God knew that if it did, all hell would break loose, and—as we have witnessed in the centuries since then—it has done just that.

FREEDOM INCLUDES RESPONSIBILITY

Prior to sin entering the world, Adam and Eve were instructed to get information in life and to live with that knowledge according to the government of the garden. After sin came into the world, God turned the government over to mankind allowing now for the entrance of illegitimate bondage, thus expanding the original intention of the concept of freedom to include a release from such bondage. However, the underlying principle for living life fully remained the same: maximum freedom coupled with limited regulation, as well as swift and significant consequences for breaking the restrictions.

It is essential to note that inclusive in biblical freedom is personal responsibility. Let's look back at verse 15 where it says, "Then the LORD God took the man and put him into the garden of Eden *to cultivate it and keep it*." Freedom didn't simply offer responsibility; it required it. God gave Adam all of the raw materials necessary to fully enjoy what He had created, but that enjoyment would come coupled with development on the part of Adam. To cultivate something is to make it productive. Cultivating involves developing its potential.

But not only was Adam instructed to cultivate the land; he was also charged with keeping it. The Hebrew word used for "keep" was *shamar*, meaning to "guard," or "have charge of."[15] At the time, the solitary threat Adam had to guard against was Satan. Spiritual warfare sought to unravel mankind as early as at our inception.

Freedom never meant that a person was to do nothing at all. Freedom meant that there was the opportunity to make a choice to exercise personal responsibility over that which God had given in order to fully maximize and realize its greatest potential. To have the opportunity to transform God's raw materials into something usable and beneficial to yourself and to others is the very essence of freedom. This is why it is crucial that civil government unleash rather than restrict freedom in society. In fact, the primary responsibility of civil government is to maintain a safe, just, and righteous environment for freedom to flourish.

Unfortunately today in our nation, we have many who cry for freedom without being willing to exercise the responsibility that comes tied to freedom. Anytime there are more people going on to government doles than there are getting jobs, something is awry and amiss in the culture. Freedom has been mistaken for something that it is not.

Society is not to erect systems whereby someone is given food stamps, donations, or financial assistance if the person is simply unwilling to work (2 Thessalonians 3:10).

In subsidizing irresponsibility we have actually lessened freedom in those who have a right to it as citizens of this great land by diminishing their motivation and opportunity to maximize their potential.

It is the obligation of freedom to fully utilize and fulfill one's assigned task through the use of God-given resources and abilities. Jesus summed up the steward who chose the easy path of hiding his talent in the ground succinctly, "You wicked, lazy slave." Then Jesus showed what is to happen to those who refuse to work. "Therefore *take away* the talent from him, and give it to the one who has the ten talents" (Matthew 25:26, 28).

The stubborn steward lost not only his own potential to live out his purpose, but he also lost the potential for his children and descendants to live out theirs because what little he did have was taken away due to his own laziness and fear.

Many in our society want the benefits of freedom while

skipping both the responsibilities and restrictions. They want God to bless America, but not one nation *under* God. However, when you extricate yourself or your society from God, you've just closed the door on freedom. Liberty is in jeopardy of being lost altogether when God is no longer part of the equation. Scripture warns that "the nations who forget God" (Psalm 9:17) will perish.

FREE TO SET FREE

Paul gives us insight into one of the primary purposes of freedom in his challenge to the church at Galatia when he admonished them to serve others—in homes, churches, and also in the communities and society at large. We read, "For you were called to freedom, brethren; only do not turn your freedom into an opportunity for the flesh, but through love serve one another" (Galatians 5:13).

You can always recognize a free person because that person is also a freedom fighter for others. God didn't give each of us the freedom that He has so that we can sit, soak, and sour. We are to use our own personal and spiritual freedoms to help enable someone else achieve the purpose that God has for him or her as well. When enough people do that in a society, the society becomes free.

Freedom exists so that freedom can exist. Freedom bequeaths freedom as those who have it seek to increase it in those who don't. One of the greatest tragedies of the Revolutionary War centered on freedom. It is true that the war itself was about freedom—freedom from the tyranny of the king's rule in England. Thirteen colonies desired to be free. Yet one of the greatest tragedies, or ironies, is that the people who fought for freedom for themselves held other people in slavery who desired and needed freedom just as much. In other words, there was a flaw in their freedom because personal freedom that does not seek freedom for others through the avenues that it can, both locally and nationally, is not freedom at all.

THE CONTRADICTION OF FREEDOM

During my college summers, I lived and worked in Philadelphia as an associate evangelist. I regularly set up tent, church, or outdoor crusades. Frequently, I was able to participate in more than the logistics of the event, but also had the opportunity to do what I am passionate about doing, and that is to posit the truth of God through preaching.

I have always been drawn to the truth. Truth, at its core, is God's view of a matter. It is a powerful entity able to transform lives both in history and for eternity. While truth includes information and facts, it also includes original intent, making it the absolute, objective standard by which reality is measured. The presence of truth brings clarity and understanding. Its absence leads to confusion and the presence of cognitive dissonance—holding contradictory ideas simultaneously.

Located in this same city of Philadelphia where I once preached as a young man is a perfect example of such a contradiction rising out of the abyss of the absence of truth. Hung in the heart of the City of Brotherly Love is the Liberty Bell. Originally cast to commemorate the fifty-year anniversary of William Penn's Charter of Privileges, the quotation, "Proclaim Liberty throughout all the land unto *all* the Inhabitants thereof" (italics added) was especially suited to the circumstances surrounding the intent of the charter and its anniversary. That quotation from Leviticus 25:10 came immediately after the command, "Consecrate the fiftieth year." It was followed by the statement, "It shall be a jubilee for you, each of you shall return to his own property, and each of you shall return to his family."

At this time in biblical history, according to this passage, all Jews who had been sold into slavery were set free (Leviticus 25:40–41). Not only was liberty a possibility in light of the Jubilee, it was guaranteed. Liberty and the end of slavery were simultaneous realities, mutually dependent upon each other in relationship to the call for jubilee.

Yet at the time in America when the jubilee was inscribed on the side of the great bell, the liberty it announced had been aborted for many. Slavery continued with no foreseeable end, sanctioned not only by society but also by the church. Fifty years after William Penn's famous charter, our nation's bell proclaimed its own contradictory fifty-year jubilee, ringing out the bittersweet sounds of an emasculated freedom across the hilltops and prairies of our vast land.

THE BREAKING OF THE BELL

My friend Ray McMillan introduced me to the Liberty Bell as a perfect object lesson for America's divides. In addressing why "the bell won't ring," Ray describes the crack as a perfect illustration for how our distortion of the Christian history of our nation has helped to maintain many divides that remain between us.

The Liberty Bell rang in celebration of momentous civic achievements or to summon people together for a special announcement. One of these achievements, according to tradition, was the first public reading of the Declaration of Independence on July 8, 1776. It is said that the sound of the Liberty Bell called out to citizens both far and near to join in this heraldic event. Rich and poor, well dressed and disheveled came together as a community to hear the words,

> We hold these truths to be self-evident, that *all* men are created equal, that they are endowed by their Creator with certain unalienable Rights, that among these

are Life, Liberty and the pursuit of Happiness. (italics added)

The Declaration's truth rang deeply within those who heard it, echoing the resonant tones of the bell. For a moment in time, both the Declaration and the Bell proclaimed liberty together. Yet fissures, or cracks, in the bell, a reflection of fissures in the conscience of our land, raised the concern of those most closely working with it. Attempts were made to bore out the cracks before they developed into something more severe.

In 1846, in honor of George Washington's birthday, the bell rang faithfully for hours until ultimately succumbing to the pressure put upon the cracks. The *Philadelphia Public Ledger* reported that just after noon, the bell split widely on one side, rendering it unringable:

> The old Independence Bell rang its last clear note on Monday last in honor of the birthday of Washington and now hangs in the great city steeple irreparably cracked and dumb. . . . It gave out clear notes and loud, and appeared to be in excellent condition until noon, when it received a sort of compound fracture in a zigzag direction through one of its sides which put it completely out of tune and left it a mere wreck of what it was.

In a city known for brotherly love, a compound fracture proclaimed otherwise. The jagged divide up the side of the symbol for equality and liberty could not be any more profound in its revelation of dualistic realities. There is a gap in the Liberty Bell, a missing point of connection preventing it from ringing clearly with the smooth tones of a complete union—of one nation under God.

Not only are we no longer one nation *under* God, we have also failed to achieve being *one* nation altogether. Whether it is reflected in racially activated acts of violence in the community, in our workplaces, in athletic realms, or in political accusations between and within parties, racism, classism, sexism, party politics, and the like simply have not been resolved. These issues smolder beneath the news headlines of the day in the areas of immigration reform, racial profiling, zoning issues, and educational disparity.

Like the problem with the bell, a compound fracture has zigzagged through our nation, keeping us largely divided along racial, class, and political lines. This division has existed for some time, and while attempts have been made to bore out the fissures through seminars, lectures, and well-intentioned efforts at creating experiences of patriotic unity, we have a long way to go toward strengthening the areas that need it or filling in the gaps that loom between us.

It is not as surprising that our nation remains divided in so many ways in our current day as it is that we, the church, have allowed so many issues to divide people of faith even more deeply than before. We cannot afford this. Our nation cannot afford this. Our sons and daughters cannot afford this. We can no longer afford to sit idly by, representing the body of Christ as a "mere wreck" of its divine design.

The solutions to the issues we face as a nation today are found only by applying a biblical and divine standard as answers to the questions before us. The church should be a model, at such a time as this, to reveal to the world what true oneness—being "one" nation or "one" church—can produce. Hell advances on the church's doorstep and our nation's doorsteps with fervent speed, and as long as we remain divided, it will continue to do so.

Our songs ring mournfully flat when the bells on our churches remain cracked.

The proof that we still have a long way to go in the church today is that a collective cross-cultural presence is not having a restorative effect in our nation. We are more concerned about achieving the American dream than we are about letting the rule of God remake segregated churches and denominations. In so doing, we have limited the degree to which the healing balm of God's grace flows freely from us into our communities, and ultimately throughout our land. If what we call freedom and oneness is not transforming individuals, families, churches, and communities, then it is merely sociology with a little Jesus sprinkled on top.

A GIFT, BUT NOT FORCED

God has demonstrated what freedom means through His original government in the garden, and He has given us the mandate of freedom—to set others free through a unified concerted effort in His name.

Society's government exists to give the boundaries for freedom, and then offer the opportunity for individuals to maximize their potential within those legitimate boundaries and be free from illegitimate bondage. If and when the government is properly protecting the freedoms of its people, then a free people are both inspired and unleashed to amplify their productivity and contribute to the freedoms of others.

What we often discover, though, throughout history, is that the further a government moves away from God and His knowledge base of truth, the more it seeks to control the lives and decisions of those it governs and limit the freedom being offered. Similar to what a cult will do, a government seeks to influence the thoughts and actions of those beneath it by restricting personal freedoms.

Freedom is an exquisite thing. But it is not a forced thing. It is important to note that while Jesus "proclaimed" the good news of the gospel and the freedom that comes from Him and the truth of God's Word, just like Lady Liberty proclaims her offer for freedom to anyone who has ears to hear, it is not forced on anyone who does not want it. Lady Liberty does not give freedom to a foreigner unless a person makes his or her way to America and goes through the process of applying for and accepting what she has to offer in order to bring her proclamation of freedom out of theory and into reality. Potential citizens must study the laws and history of the land in order to know what they are committing to. Likewise, believers in Christ need to know the Truth—study it, apply it, and practice it in order to truly experience and model the freedom that has been offered.

There is a direct correlation between the preeminence given to Christ as King in one's life and the freedom one experiences. To the degree that Jesus is exalted in personal lives, family's lives, churches, and communities is to the degree in which the rivers of freedom will flow in our nation.

It is incumbent upon the church to keep God's principles of freedom based on His truth before the civil government in a unified voice so that our nation never loses sight of God's great gift of freedom.

CHAPTER FOUR

THE NECESSITY OF BIBLICAL JUSTICE

I was in New York City in the summer of 2002 when a special ceremony was held to honor the firefighters and other rescuers who had put their lives on the line during the terrorist attacks of 9/11. It was a very serious and somber ceremony as the city remembered all those who lost their lives seeking to rescue others on that terrible day because they were in a life-and-death situation.

We have all heard the stories of people who laid aside their own comfort and safety and took great risks to save lives or to improve others' chances at experiencing life. Those rescuers knew they could not simply stand by and watch people perish. There was too much at stake to be casual about the situation. The 9/11 rescuers mobilized themselves because they knew that many people would either live or die based on their efforts.

People who are facing certain disaster need a rescuer to lead them out of harm's way, no matter what the cost or inconvenience to the rescuer. And people who are facing certain spiritual disaster without Jesus Christ also need someone to lead them to safety, which is to the cross of Jesus Christ where sin is paid for and forgiven. Yet God has asked us to do even more. There are people facing certain social disasters—who are struggling to make it, can't catch a break, need food, housing, an opportunity, or more, and we as a nation have positioned ourselves to be that place where people can discover a way out.

The kingdom agenda involves promoting freedom in a nation through the vehicle of what is often called, in our contemporary society, *social justice*. However, social justice has become a convoluted term meaning different things to different people. It is often used as a catchphrase for illegitimate forms of government that promote the redistribution of wealth as well as the collectivistic expansion of civil government, which wrongly infringes on the jurisdictions of God's other covenantal institutions (family and church).

Such a view of social justice is a contradiction and denial of biblical justice, since biblical justice seeks to protect individual liberty while promoting personal responsibility. For example, the biblical injunction of "Thou shalt not steal" includes areas such as government-sanctioned theft through state-enforced redistribution of wealth and illegitimate taxation.

For our purposes in these pages, the term I have chosen to use is *biblical justice* rather than social justice, because biblical justice provides society with a divine frame of reference from which to operate.

The word *justice* in Scripture means to prescribe the right way, and it is the cornerstone of God's rule (Psalm 89:14). Since God is just (Deuteronomy 32:4) and is the ultimate lawgiver (James 4:12), His laws and judgments are just and righteous (Psalms 19:7–9; 111:7–8). They are to be applied without partiality (Exodus 23:3, 6; Deuteronomy 1:17; Leviticus 19:15; Numbers 15:16), seeing as justice identifies the moral standard by which God measures human conduct (Isaiah 26:7). It is the government's role, then, to be His instrument of divine justice by impartially establishing, reflecting, and applying His divine standards of justice in society (Psalm 72:1–2, 4; 2 Samuel 8:15; Deuteronomy 4:7–8).

Biblical justice, therefore, is *the equitable and impartial application of the rule of God's moral law in society*. Whether exercising itself through economic, political, social, or criminal justice, the one constant within all four realms is the understanding and application of God's moral law within the social realm.

THE SPIRITUAL AND THE SOCIAL

It is the division of the sacred and the secular that has led to the cultural disintegration we are now experiencing in our nation. It was never the Creator's desire to have such a separation exist in His world. From Genesis to Revelation, it is inextricably clear that the spiritual and the social are always to be integrated if life is to be lived the way God intended.

In fact, the Bible expressly states that the reason there is social disintegration in the form of all kinds of immorality and domestic and international chaos is that man wrongfully segregates the spiritual from the social (2 Chronicles 15:3–6). When God created man, man was given the responsibility to rule the earth under divine authority while simultaneously spreading God's image throughout the world (Genesis 1:26–28).

However, it was man's refusal to submit to divine authority that led to the first social disintegration. When man disobeyed God, the result was family breakdown, economic struggle, emotional instability, and physical death (Genesis 3:1–19). The more clearly God's rule is reflected in society, the more ordered society will be.

When God established Israel, He wrote their constitution in the form of the Ten Commandments. These commandments were divided between man's vertical responsibility to God and his horizontal responsibility to his neighbor. Consequently, God deemed the spiritual and social relationship necessary for the proper functioning of society (Exodus 20:1–17). God also wanted His people to reflect His character through charitable works and acts of kindness to people outside of Israel as a reflection of their gratitude for His goodness to them (Deuteronomy 10:17–19).

Biblical justice is not a man-made, socially imposed, top-down system ultimately leading to the negation of freedom. Biblical justice promotes freedom through emphasizing accountability, equality, and responsibility in providing a spiritual underpinning in the social realms.

Each of the four jurisdictions in God's kingdom—individual, family, church, and civil government—is called upon to promote justice and responsibility under God in its own distinct way. Through these jurisdictions, God has given man the task of impartially protecting the "unalienable rights" He has granted to each of us. One way this is done is through the just removal of illegitimate boundaries that prohibit people from pursuing and fully experiencing all that God has created them to be.

GOD THE DELIVERER

Repeatedly throughout Scripture, God has revealed Himself as a defender and deliverer. The Exodus out of Egypt dramatically portrays God's execution of biblical justice on behalf of a group of people who were oppressed. Later, when God gave His laws to Israel, He reminded them of His deliverance. He said, "You shall not wrong a stranger or oppress him, for you were strangers in the land of Egypt" (Exodus 22:21).

God regularly tied either a presence or an absence of biblical justice to a presence or absence of His blessing. For example, Israel's worship was rejected because of an absence of justice in society (Amos 5:21–24). The Israelites were taken into captivity and held in bondage because of their rebellion against God. God had repeatedly told them to turn from their sin and practice "justice and righteousness," pay back what was stolen, and secure every pledge (Ezekiel 33:10–33).

The destruction of Sodom and Gomorrah, as another example, is often attributed to the blatant practice of homosexuality; however, God clearly links His wrath toward them to their lack of concern for the poor (Ezekiel 16:49).

The prophets of the Old Testament regularly condemned the people for their social injustices as well. These social condemnations were not merely viewed as secular affronts to communities, but also a spiritual affront to God (Zechariah 7:9–12). God's people were specifically instructed to seek the welfare of the secular city in which they were living and to pray for its well-being so that it would become a better place to live, work, and raise their families (Jeremiah 29:4–7).

Therefore, the role of believers, and believers who make up the nation, is to seek for the means to execute divine justice on behalf of the defenseless, poor, and oppressed. Scripture relates biblical justice distinctly to these groups as a primary concern because it is these groups that most represent the helpless in society and bear the brunt of injustices.

We have been instructed not to mistreat the poor (James 2:15–16) or to have class and racial prejudice (Galatians 2:11–14). Rather, we are commissioned to meet the physical needs of the "have nots" in a responsible way. The Bible is clear on spiritual ministry and social responsibility working hand-in-hand. When the two are properly connected and integrated, people become productive citizens of society while also becoming prepared for life in eternity.

LOVING GOD, LOVING OTHERS

A strong biblical connection exists between our knowledge and relationship with God and our concern for the poor and the oppressed (Jeremiah 22:16; Matthew 25:40). Micah 6:8 reveals this, "He has told you, O man, what is good; And what does the LORD require of you But to do justice, to love kindness, And to walk humbly with your God?" We *do justice* in a humble relation to a just God as a natural reflection of His presence in our lives. Religion becomes authentic when it manifests itself in ministry to others in need.

A primary focus in Scripture is concern for the poor. More than three hundred verses directly relate to the treatment of the poor, strategies to aid the poor, God's intentions for the poor, and what our perspective should be toward the poor. Space doesn't allow us to go through all of them, but the point is clear that God cares about the poor particularly because they are the most vulnerable to suffering from injustice.

Ultimately, *doing justice* fulfills the two greatest commandments given to us by Jesus—that of loving God and loving others (Matthew 22:37–40). Christ says, "On these two commandments depend the whole Law and the Prophets." Both the content and meaning of the Law and Prophets were centered not only on one's relationship to God, but also on whether one was rightly related to his neighbor. The implication is that understanding of and love for God that does not also express itself in love for one's neighbor does not satisfy the biblical definition of love.

Thus, Jesus linked our attitude toward God (spiritual) with our attitude toward others (social). When a lawyer asked "Who is my neighbor [that I am to love?]," Jesus responded by telling the story of the Good Samaritan, pointing out that your neighbor is the person whose need you see and whose need you are able to meet (Luke 10:26–37). Jesus concludes the story by exhorting us to love in like manner.

It is important to note the meaning of love because we often confuse love with an emotion. While love can contain emotions, the Greek word used in this command to love God and love others is the word *agape*. It is not referring to "liking" someone or preferring a certain personality. Love is *compassionately and righteously pursuing the well-being of another.* Jesus used the condition of injustice as an intrinsic aspect to a proper perception of defining the meaning of loving one's neighbor. Therefore, since loving one's neighbor includes seeking his best interest by relieving him from injustice or oppression when it is necessary and we are able, love for God is validated through a liberating love for others.

Jesus' earthly ministry consistently modeled the integration of the spiritual and the social that He taught about in that He dwelt among the oppressed (Luke 5:1–11), ate with them (Luke 5:27–32), comforted them (Luke 12:22–34), fed them (Luke 9:10–17), restored them (Luke 5:12–16), and ministered to them (Luke 7:18–23) in fulfillment of His Father's will. All of Jesus' good works were clearly connected to the spiritual purposes of God (Matthew 4:23–24).

When Jesus gave His great Sermon on the Mount, He instructed His disciples to be the salt of the earth and light to the world (Matthew 5:13–16). Salt was used as a preservative to stop decay, and light was used to dispel darkness. Christ's followers were to influence society for God, accomplished by the good works they did for others in the name of God. Therefore, good works done for the benefit of helping people must include, not exclude, God. Good works originate from God, are done through God, and align under the truth of God in order to bring glory to God. In other words, God gets the credit for everything. Good works are not good words, nor are they simply good things. You don't have to be a Christian to do good things. The unsaved can build orphanages and houses, give money, visit the sick, and do a lot of other good things. But what the unsaved cannot do is glorify God through good works. Good works must always be tied to God's glory.

The apostle John also stressed the connection between love for God and love for others when he said, "If someone says, 'I love God,' and hates his brother, he is a liar; for the one who does not love his brother whom he has seen, cannot love God whom he has not seen" (1 John 4:20). John reminded us that this love is to be expressed through actions and not just words, as it is carried out in "deed and truth" (1 John 3:18).

Further emphasis that this love should be given to the poor and oppressed as special objects of God's concern comes when James writes, "Did not God choose the poor of this world to be rich in faith and heirs of the kingdom which He promised to those who love Him?" (James 2:5). He also defines true religion by how one treats the widow and the orphan (James 1:27).

This same emphasis continued within the operation of the early church. As a result, the influence of the first century church was so powerful in society that it brought great joy to the entire city (Acts 8:8) and was said to have turned the world upside down (Acts 17:6). The church became known for its good works (Acts 4:32–35; 5:11–16). Members of the church were taught to do good, not only to other church members but also to all people (Galatians 6:10).

Biblical justice isn't simply a ministry to be relegated to a special event. Biblical justice is a foundational part of fulfilling the purpose of the church and church members in having an impact in the nation, as intimated by the heart of God. It is a result of God's people becoming one through being what God has called us to be and participating in what He has called us to do—*justice*.

JUSTICE AND THE GOSPEL

There is some confusion today about the implications of the gospel, and to what degree the gospel includes this mandate of justice. It is unfortunate that the term *gospel* has been reduced to only referring to the plan of salvation today. This limited understanding and use of the term has allowed people to be concerned about people's souls for eternity and ignore their well-being in history.

Some Christians believe that to include social liberation and justice in the gospel is to preach a "different gospel." Others believe that to exclude social liberation and justice as part of the gospel is to deny the gospel. Black liberation theology was formed on this latter thesis.

To resolve this dilemma we need to make a distinction between the gospel's content and its scope. This distinction is important because through it is determined the extent that we are to "do justice" as the church, as part of our comprehensive responsibility of proclaiming the gospel in an effort to transform our nation.

THE SCOPE OF THE GOSPEL

The content of the gospel message is limited and contained. Paul made this unmistakably clear in 1 Corinthians when he said,

> Now I make known to you, brethren, the gospel which I preached to you, which also you received, in which also you stand, by which also you are saved, if you hold fast the word which I preached to you, unless you believed in vain. For I delivered to you as of first importance what I also received, that Christ died for our sins according to the Scriptures, and that He was buried, and that He was raised on the third day according to the Scriptures. (1 Corinthians 15:1–4)

Clearly, the content of the gospel message is the death, burial, and resurrection of Jesus Christ. Scripture is plain that it is personal faith in the finished work of Christ that brings people the forgiveness of sin, a personal relationship with God, and eternal life. It is through believing the gospel that Christians access God's grace, or unmerited favor, for every area of their life.

The gospel's scope, however, reaches further into sanctification, within which are located the concepts of justice and social action. We see this scope in Paul's use of the word *gospel* when he informs the Christians in Rome that by the "gospel" they are established (Romans 16:25). Likewise, in the book of Romans the gospel is called "the power of God for salvation" (1:16), and is said to include "the righteousness of God . . . revealed from faith to faith" (v. 17). This righteousness includes sanctification, since "the righteous man shall live by faith" (Habakkuk 2:4; Romans 1:17).

In addition, the gospel is viewed as the criterion of Christian conduct (Philippians 1:27), and believers are viewed as being obedient to the gospel when they are active in the ministry of love to poorer believers (2 Corinthians 9:13). Paul further exemplified that the gospel involves more than the preliminary reception of salvation, but also a life of liberty, freedom, and multi-racial relationships, when he rebuked Peter for drawing distinctions between Gentiles and Jews on the basis of circumcision. Paul said that in doing so Peter had not been "straightforward about the truth of the gospel" (Galatians 2:14). So here again, the word "gospel" is not used just in concert with eternal destiny but also with racial unity within the body of Christ.

The gospel also encompasses the whole man as directly

stated by Paul, "Now may the God of peace Himself sanctify you entirely; and may your spirit and soul and body be preserved complete" (1 Thessalonians 5:23). A view of mankind that divides the invisible world (soul) from the visible world (body) narrows the understanding of the scope of the gospel. This is reflected in a desire to save people's souls, thus compartmentalizing a section of man; that is, to save an aspect of man as opposed to the man himself.

This division between the immaterial and material parts of man leads to a lack of application by way of biblical justice through emphasizing the spiritual over the social. However, the relationship of the soul to the body is to be seen as a unified whole. Biblical terms referring to the spiritual aspects of man support this reference to man's whole person, including the body. The Hebrew word for soul (*nephesh*) refers to the whole person, which includes the body (Genesis 2:7; Lamentations 3:24; Genesis 46:18). Another word for soul (*ruach*) is also used to refer to the whole man (Isaiah 26:9). In the New Testament, the Greek word for soul (*psuche*) is used to refer to Christ's body, seeing as souls do not die and go to the grave (Acts 2:27, 29).

Therefore, church members are commissioned to deliver the content of the gospel (evangelism) so that people come into a personal relationship with God. Yet the church is also commissioned to live out the scope of the gospel (sanctification) so that people can realize the full manifestation of it and glorify God. The content of the gospel produces oneness in the church as we evangelize the world together. The scope also produces oneness through good works that are based on the principles of biblical justice.

JESUS AND THE GOSPEL

The greatest illustration of both the content and scope of the gospel is found in Luke chapter 4. This passage took place at a time when the Jews were living in social and economic oppression under Rome. The Jews hated the domination of the Romans, were looking for a Messiah to deliver them, and desperately wanted their freedom.

Roaming the hillsides at that time was a man named Barabbas. Barabbas was a leader of a group of counter-revolutionaries known as the zealots. These zealots wreaked havoc along the Judean hills in order to protest and resist Roman imperialism and oppression. Caught in the middle of one of these pillaging raids, Barabbas was eventually arrested and sentenced to death on a cross.

Jesus was a contemporary of Barabbas. Jesus was known at that time as a man of no reputation who had been born in a tiny country town called Bethlehem. While news had begun to spread about Him around the other parts of the country, His greatest claim to fame in His hometown of Nazareth was that He was the son of a carpenter.

One day, Jesus had returned to Nazareth. As was the custom when there was a visitor, He was given the opportunity to read the Scripture and offer the morning's commentary. Having been handed the book of Isaiah, Jesus turned to the place in Isaiah that He wanted to read. We know that He purposefully turned there because Scripture records that He "found the place where it was written . . ." (Luke 4:17). Jesus looked for a particular passage that would deliver a particular truth at a particular time to a particular audience with a particular need. He did so because he had a particular point that He wanted to make. When He found the passage he was looking for, He read,

> THE SPIRIT OF THE LORD IS UPON ME, BECAUSE HE ANOINTED ME TO PREACH THE GOSPEL TO THE POOR. HE HAS SENT ME TO PROCLAIM RELEASE TO THE CAPTIVES, AND RECOVERY OF SIGHT TO THE BLIND, TO SET FREE THOSE WHO ARE OPPRESSED, TO PROCLAIM THE FAVORABLE YEAR OF THE LORD. (Luke 4:18–19)

Then "He closed the book, gave it back to the attendant and sat down; and the eyes of all in the synagogue were fixed on Him. And He began to say to them, 'Today this Scripture has been fulfilled in your hearing'" (Luke 4:20–21).

Don't overlook that Jesus said, "*Today* this . . . has been fulfilled." The timing of the reading of this passage is crucial.

Jesus intentionally chose this passage at a time when the Jews were in the middle of an economic, political, and social crisis. He came on the scene in the midst of a society experiencing the devastating effects of injustice and said that the Spirit of the Lord was upon Him to proclaim good news: the gospel.

What is essential to note from this passage is that Jesus Himself said that He had good news (the gospel) for those in the economic crisis—*the poor*. He had good news (the gospel) for those in the political crisis—*the captives*. He had good news (the gospel) for those in the social crisis—*the oppressed*. This good news that He had was the gospel of the favorable year of the Lord.

THE DAY OF ATONEMENT

The "favorable year" is also known as the Jubilee, as briefly mentioned in the previous chapter. To understand it more fully, we need to look at the contextual framework in which it first appeared. We read in Leviticus,

> You shall then sound a ram's horn abroad on the tenth day of the seventh month; on the day of atonement you shall sound a horn all through your land. You shall thus consecrate the fiftieth year and proclaim a release through the land to all its inhabitants. It shall be a jubilee for you. (Leviticus 25:9–10)

The Year of Jubilee, as noted in this passage, was inaugurated with the Day of Atonement. This was the day set aside to atone for the sins of the nation of Israel both individually and corporately. The Day of Atonement was when Israel got right with God through the shedding of blood—the slaying of a sacrifice. In other words, they didn't get the Jubilee (i.e., God's involvement economically, socially, and politically—an aspect of the scope of the gospel) without first getting their sins addressed by God (a type reflecting the future content of the gospel). They didn't get the social until they had the spiritual. If they skipped the Day of Atonement in order to get the social benefits of the Jubilee, they lost out on the Jubilee altogether because there was a prescribed method for how God instituted His agenda.

A common problem we find in our nation today is that many people want God to do things for them without the Day of Atonement. A lot of people cry for justice or for God to pay this, fix that, redeem this, or vindicate that while skipping the very thing that inaugurates God's Jubilee—which is the addressing of personal and corporate sin. God's wrath against sin must always be addressed, which in the dispensation of the church comes through our relationship with Jesus Christ, before He is free to give the social freedom we are looking for. If the spiritual is not foundational, there isn't going to be a Jubilee.

The reason that the Jews didn't receive the freedom that

Jesus proclaimed to them was that they rejected Him and His atonement. They wanted the social action without the spiritual interaction. However, Jubilee came as the result of the atonement.

Jesus proclaimed good news. He proclaimed the gospel. He proclaimed release for the captives and sight for the blind. He didn't force it by eradicating capitalism and developing a spiritualized socialism. He simply offered it under the condition that it must be accepted through a prescribed atonement before it can be experienced.

Jesus couldn't give Jubilee to the Jews because they refused to deal with their sin and receive Him as their Messiah. Jesus would have provided them with the deliverance from Rome they so greatly desired, if they had recognized Him as their future atonement and their Lord. However, the Jews wanted the benefits of the Messiah without the relationship with the Messiah. But that's not how God's justice works.

No guarantee of deliverance exists without first addressing the spiritual through the atonement.

CHRIST AS KING

Many of the Jews witnessed Jesus feeding thousands and healing the sick, but they demanded that He be crucified in exchange for the release of the rebel leader Barabbas. They chose the revolutionary who was attempting to free them from Roman bondage via a revolution, not the One who would do it via the cross. This is because they only wanted a welfare program rather than to be made well through spiritual transformation. They wanted deliverance but not the King who delivers. And ever since then, mankind has been trying, and failing, to solve the problems of our societies in like manner, not via the favorable year of the Lord through the Day of Atonement, which is the supremacy of the gospel of Jesus Christ.

Jesus' ministry gave the proper order for how to approach all issues of justice and social action. He could have snapped His fingers and delivered all of the poor, the widows, and the oppressed. Instead, He was very particular about His involvement. He became involved in connection with the proclamation of His kingdom message. His purpose was to provide not only physical freedom and relief, but spiritual as well, because He knew that the spiritual and the physical are connected with each other.

Jesus' gospel, as recorded in Luke 4, is the good news that includes both the spiritual and the physical. To make His proclamation merely social is not good news. If a person has the best food to eat, the nicest clothes to wear, and the greatest job at which to work, and yet still dies without a relationship with Christ through His atonement, he doesn't have anything at all.

But to make His proclamation merely spiritual is not the

full experience of "good news" either. To tell a person that Jesus can give him a home in heaven but that He can't do anything about where he lives on earth—or to tell him that he's got shoes, I've got shoes, and all of God's children have shoes in heaven but that we all have to go barefoot on earth isn't all that good of news either.

Jesus' gospel includes both the spiritual and the social. It is designed to build God's kingdom rather than try to save our nation's systems. It is designed to provide a model of a different system, one created by God, which provides a divine alternative so that our nation can see what God can do in broken humanity. All of the social activity in our country cannot solve our country's problems. In the long term, social action is limited; lasting solutions can only come from the kingdom of God because that's where the atonement guarantees lasting freedom.

Unless social action is based on spiritual discipleship, it will lack the power for long-term transformation. This is because there is a spiritual reality behind every physical problem. By addressing the underlying theological or spiritual issues, along with the physical, we can achieve long-term solutions because we have addressed the entire problem, not just its physical manifestation. Secular society does not understand the spiritual reality that causes physical, social, political, and economic problems. Therefore, secular society is limited in its ability to impact and transform land.

IMPLEMENTING BIBLICAL JUSTICE

God has a vision. His vision is His kingdom agenda. The kingdom agenda is God's methodology for impacting and transforming the world in which we live.

God's vision promises hope both for time and eternity to all who will receive it, by connecting the social with the spiritual in a biblically based frame of reference. The social without the spiritual may help people temporarily but leave them impoverished for eternity. The spiritual without the social may have people looking forward to a great eternity but missing what God wants to do to, through, and for people in history. As we have seen, both are essential for the transformation of not only individuals, families, and churches, but also our nation.

There are three key principles for implementing biblical justice we need to enact: restitution, reconciliation, and responsibility. Much can be accomplished when like-minded individuals embrace one another's strengths to work together toward a shared vision of promoting biblical justice in our society.

BIBLICAL JUSTICE AND RESTITUTION

If the principles of biblical justice were implemented in our society today, we wouldn't have prisons full to overflowing.

This is because the aim of biblical justice is always a cessation of the crime coupled, when possible, with restitution to the victim.

In biblical times, this was carried out in one of three ways: capital, corporal, or economic punishment. Capital punishment addressed heinous offenders by applying the death penalty to severe crimes. Corporal punishment regulated a controlled form of physical punishment, along with the potential for restitution (Exodus 21:22–25, 28–30). Economic punishment put economic justice into effect through the repayment with interest of what had been lost through the crime (Exodus 22:1–3).

Regardless of the arena of application, biblical restitution was always specific to the offended victim. It included a designated amount that had a predetermined end for when full restitution would be realized and forgiveness granted (Leviticus 6:1–7). If these guidelines had been used for our modern-day institution of affirmative action, we would not have gotten burdened down in endless debates regarding its effectiveness and conclusion.

While governments have a crucial part to play in delivering justice, what we as the body of Christ need to remember is that God did not create governments to take care of the things He has called the church to do. Christians should be representing God's kingdom by caring for people across racial, gender, political, and class lines so well that government experts come to us to find out how we do it. Jesus could feed, heal, lead, and minister to people in a way that was a witness to the world. Because He was able to minister to their needs, Jesus turned the people's eyes toward Him and not toward the Roman government.

BIBLICAL JUSTICE AND RECONCILIATION

Not only does biblical justice focus on restitution, but it also comes tempered with the potential for mercy toward the offender. The cross of Jesus Christ is the greatest example of this appeal for mercy. While on the cross, Jesus asked His Father to forgive those who were killing Him (Luke 23:34). Through the parable of the two slaves who owed money, Jesus teaches that this principle of mercy should govern how we treat others as well (Matthew 18:21–34).

While mercy is not always granted in the execution of justice, the opportunity for it makes biblical justice distinct. This should cause each of us to be grateful, because without God's mercy, none of us would be here today. It should also cause each of us to be willing to extend mercy, when able, as an outgrowth of having received it ourselves.

When combining restitution with mercy, biblical justice then has the unique ability to lead toward reconciliation as well. A secular example of this combination happened in South Africa. Following Apartheid, South Africa initiated what has come to be known as the model of Truth Commissions throughout the country. Newly elected President Nelson Mandela established the Truth and Reconciliation Commission (TRC) as a court-like restorative justice body tasked with discovering, revealing, and, inasmuch as possible, righting past wrongdoing by a government in the hope of fostering reconciliation through resolving conflict, and its resultant consequences, left over from the past.

The key term in the Commission was "reconciliation." Justice was sought, in this case, toward the end goal of reconciliation, leading South Africa to stand head and shoulders above other nations in its bid for cooperation and oneness within its governing institutions.

The United States government has never enacted a Truth and Reconciliation Commission for the injustices committed by the founding members of our nation, as well as those who came after them, toward African-Americans. These injustices lie largely in the past, but they do not lie dormant. Their tremors and repercussions remain as alive and active as ever, as evidenced in the societal schisms still present in our country today.

Biblical justice does not simply mean halting an evil that has been done to a group of people. Biblical justice is willing to also offer restitution and reconciliation to the victim in order to salve the psychologically, sociologically, and spiritually inflicted wounds as the evil's result. Biblical justice contains much more than an awareness of a past wrong, and its cessation.

BIBLICAL JUSTICE AND RESPONSIBILITY

Seldom in the discussion of the poor or biblical justice do we hear the word *empowerment*, a risky term simply because couched within it is another word: *power*. Human nature rarely lends itself to relinquishing power to another person whether it is done relationally, socially, spiritually, or politically.

In fact, the words often associated with the poor and social action in our contemporary language involve concepts such as relief, charity, and aid. The focus is on how to make life more palatable for the poor through temporal and often inadequate provisions of a meal, clothing, or housing. While well-intentioned and helpful in many ways, this often nurtures a paternalistic style of justice, causing us to forget that we are not our brother's keeper but that we are our brother's brother. Rather, we need to seek to give the poor the power that they need to ultimately rise above their situation into a position of personal responsibility.

Injustice is not simply mistreating the poor or oppressing others. Injustice involves a refusal to appropriately equip and empower the defenseless, poor, and oppressed in such a way so as to maximize their productive potential. Therefore, one of the primary purposes of biblical justice and social action should always be the creation of productivity that ultimately empowers people, calling them to take personal responsibility.

In Scripture, charity was essentially an opportunity to work. This is illustrated by the process of gleaning, which we touched on earlier, whereby the needy could collect the overlooked, cast off, and leftover grain that God's people were expected to leave behind from their harvest for the benefit of the poor (Leviticus 19:9–10; Deuteronomy 24:17–22). Through taking responsibility for being productive, people could turn poverty into productivity in response to the charitable opportunities provided by others.

Gleaning provided the opportunity for the poor to help themselves out of poverty while simultaneously upholding their dignity since they were participants in the system and not merely passive recipients of charity. The harder a person worked, even as a poor person, the more productive that individual became.

This is why a just and righteous free market economy, *biblical economics*, is the best system, because it provides the incentive for the producers of wealth to maximize their abilities while concurrently encouraging responsibility through empowering forms of charity for those who have the ability to work.

Other economic systems that stifle, limit, and illegitimately control the ways and means of production not only hinder economic growth but also limit the authentic expression of biblical charity. These systems produce government-run welfare states that keep people trapped in the very poverty and oppression that they say they are seeking to eliminate. The economic responsibility of civil government is to remove fraud and coercion from the marketplace, thus keeping it free from tyranny. It is not to control the marketplace (statism). Centralized governmental control of trade is the economic system of the Antichrist (Revelation 13:17).

Another purpose of biblical justice and social action, along with empowerment, is the impartation of knowledge. Knowledge is one of the greatest tools that can be given to people to either lift themselves out of, or defend themselves within, a situation of injustice. The clearest biblical example of the benefits of knowledge in an unjust situation is demonstrated in the book of Esther. We often read the story of Esther with a focus on the beauty of Esther as a heroine who rescued her people from certain death. However, Esther didn't rescue her people from certain death at all. She merely enabled her people to defend themselves from the threat of certain death through the knowledge of the upcoming battle, along with the right to bear arms (Esther 8:11).

The law of the land forbade the king from reversing the order he had made to exterminate all of the Jews in his nation. What the Jews gained through Esther's stand was the knowledge of the ensuing battle, which allowed them the time to amass and use arms to legally defend themselves from their oppressor. Esther didn't win the battle for her people; she simply gave her people the ability to fight for themselves.

Knowledge empowers. However, if the statistics from our schools are any indicator, a large number of our young people are failing to be empowered today. In three of our nation's major cities—Detroit, Baltimore, and New York City—less than 40 percent of all high school students will graduate. And yet our churches sit idly by, housing the largest, most qualified volunteer force in the nation who can both infiltrate and impact our society for good.

Churches exist in every community. Therefore the structure to address social problems is already in place. The church is ideally suited to serve as a unified force for change. Only we have misunderstood our calling. As we often do when reading the story of Esther, we have become enchanted by the beauty within the safety of our own four walls to such a degree that we have forgotten that there is a battle upon us.

We live in a nation that has been called post-Christian. So how is our society going to know what God's law is and how it is supposed to function? Let me answer that from Scripture. In Deuteronomy 4:5–6, Moses cautioned the Israelites that when they entered Canaan, they were to obey God's "statutes and judgments" as given to Moses.

By so doing, Israel would be a testimony to the unbelieving nations around them who would look at Israel and say, "Surely this great nation is a wise and understanding people" (v. 6c).

Then Moses went on to explain why the nations would say this: "For what great nation is there that has a god so near to it as is the LORD our God whenever we call on Him? Or what great nation is there that has statutes and judgments as righteous as this whole law which I am setting before you today?" (Deuteronomy 4:7–8).

Our nation will know what true justice looks like when the people of God demonstrate the equitable application of God's law within the spheres of influence God has given. Finally, how does a kingdom agenda of biblical justice work itself out in society? Psalm 72 says:

> Give the Your judgments, O God, And Your righteousness to the king's son. May he judge Your people with righteousness and Your afflicted with justice.
> . . . May he vindicate the afflicted of the people, Save the children of the needy And crush the oppressor.
> (vv. 1–2, 4)

The job of civil government is to function as an instrument of God's justice. But once government no longer sees itself as God's agent under His authority, it becomes its own humanistic institution. Then the vote of the majority guides the decisions, or else decisions are made by those who have the most power. In either case, the result cannot be a just and righteous society.

That is why we need committed kingdom-minded Christians running for political office. I'm not just talking about people who are saved and on their way to heaven but people who have developed a theistic worldview, a God-centered orientation that they bring to every area of public life.

We also need committed young Christians in fields such as law; we need honest people who hold to God's standard of truth and justice and will do things God's way, not necessarily the cultural way.

We need people in places of influence who can bring divine justice to bear on this society. When unrighteous people rule, there is no moral law. When there is no moral law, there is no presence of God. And when there is no presence of God, there is a nation in chaos.

Only as believers function under and promote the governing bodies operating in accordance with the rule of God will we begin to fully experience God's hand of blessing and providence on our land once again. When our institutions carry out their duties under God's rule, that is when the freedom that God wants us to have as a nation will be truly possible. Kingdom-minded Christians living all of life under the kingdom agenda and bringing that influence to bear into the culture is what our country needs to bring us back as the dominant force for good as we once were in so many ways, not only internally but around the world.

CONCLUSION

One of the most well-known phrases in the English language occurs in our very own Declaration of Independence. In the definitive statement of freedom by those escaping oppression and monarchic rule, key values were etched into validation and preservation through these words. We read,

> We hold these truths to be self-evident, that all men are created equal, that they are endowed by their Creator with certain unalienable Rights, *that among these are Life, Liberty and the pursuit of Happiness.* (italics added)

This phrase outlining our inalienable rights as "Life, Liberty and the pursuit of Happiness" is one of the most widely recognized statements in our written history.

The reason why it has not become lost in the dusty annals on our shelves is because its profundity resonates intrinsically within each of us. It speaks to us in a manner that communicates not only with our minds but also with our souls. It talks of the destiny and purpose that God has planted within each of us as His treasured creation. Not only that, it shouts loudly concerning God's foundational tie to the inception of a government designed to protect the freedoms of those governed. When God is removed or diminished, our undeniable rights are in jeopardy.

Yet what is unfortunate today is that we have somehow moved away from this foundation. We have distanced, and in some cases removed, ourselves from the basis for who we are and why we were created as a nation. We have strayed from the prescribed foundation that our government was designed to defend against the threats on our basic unalienable rights, as well as to promote and increase the opportunities for our rights. And instead, as believers, we have lost ourselves in a whole other question: Is God a democrat or a republican?

This is largely due to the reality that our political battles today revolve less around principles, or even the policies to foster those principles, as they do around politics. Democrats and republicans have become deeply split by particular political orientations, oftentimes ushering in deadlock for the sake of deadlock. This results in the same productivity level you would achieve on a football team where five players rushed toward one goal line and the remaining six players on the team rushed to the other. As such, we as a nation are suffering underneath the spending of an inordinate amount of money as reflected in our national deficit and debt with a less-than-adequate amount of forward progress to show for it.

Yet where does God fall on this issue of partisan politics? Is God a Democrat or a Republican? Whose side is He on? In order to answer that question, as we conclude our time together in this booklet, we need to turn to a battle that took place under Joshua's military and governmental leadership.

In Joshua chapter five, Joshua had crossed into the Promised Land and was now serving as the one in charge over the nation of Israel. Although God had declared that He would give the land to the Israelites, His promises needed to be made manifest through certain processes. In other words, what God had promised needed to be actualized through different battles, conquests, and wars.

One of these battles that took place happened at the city of Jericho. Now, when I mention the Battle of Jericho, you can most likely recount certain aspects of the battle such as the armies marching undefended around the city, the priests blowing the trumpets, and the walls falling down. But there is one critical scenario that took place just near Jericho that is frequently ignored in our Bible lessons and even in our sermons. And yet this critical scenario sheds a revealing light on how a Christian should vote.

Prior to the battle and like any military leader should, Joshua performed reconnaissance. Facing what appeared to be an impregnable wall and an invisible culture, Joshua set out to determine how best to secure his victory. As Joshua prepared to go to war against the city of Jericho, a representative of God's army approached him. Joshua then asked him a very practical and strategic question. I'll paraphrase:

> Whose side are you on? Are you on our side or are you on their side?

In other words, "Are you a Democrat or a Republican?"

What happened next is a game-changer. The commander of the Lord's army gave what is perhaps the most politically insightful principle in Scripture when he replied, again in the Evans translation,

> Neither. I'm not on your side and I'm not on their side. I'm on God's side.

We read in Joshua 5,

> Now it came about when Joshua was by Jericho, that he lifted up his eyes and looked, and behold, a man was standing opposite him with his sword drawn in

his hand, and Joshua went to him and said to him,
"Are you for us or for our adversaries?" He said, "*No;
rather I indeed come now as captain of the host of the
Lord.*"

The captain of the host of the Lord made it clear that he
hadn't come to take sides. He had come to take over. He was
not on Joshua's side, yet neither was he on Jericho's side.
However, Joshua could have easily assumed that he would
have sided with him since Joshua was on the side with the
chosen people of God. After all, that would make sense. Yet
the captain made it clear: He was on God's side.

He did not align himself with Joshua's agenda nor with
Jericho's. He aligned himself with a whole other agenda, that
of God's kingdom. Sometimes that would play out in favor of
Joshua—as in the battle at Jericho. Yet sometimes that would
not play out in favor of Joshua—as we read just a chapter
later in the battle of Ai. The reason why the Israelites were
defeated at Ai wasn't because God took the side of Ai. It was,
again because God took His own side—His own kingdom
side—and Joshua's people had gone against it (see Joshua
chapter 7).

God is not merely a God of Democrats. Nor is He merely a
God of Republicans. God does not ride the backs of donkeys
or elephants. Like the captain of the Lord's army, He didn't
come to take sides; He came to take over.

As a nation, we can either side with the One who is truly in charge and experience victory— like at Jericho. Or we can choose our own way and experience defeat—like at Ai. Unless we continue to strive to be one nation under God, as we were when we were first founded, we will fail to be one nation over much of anything at all.

THE URBAN ALTERNATIVE

Dr. Tony Evans and The Urban Alternative (TUA) equips, empowers, and unites Christians to impact individuals, families, churches, and communities to restore hope and transform lives.

We believe the core cause of the problems we face in our personal lives, homes, churches, and societies is a spiritual one; therefore, the only way to address them is spiritually. We've tried a political, a social, an economic, and even a religious agenda. It's time for a Kingdom Agenda—God's visible and comprehensive rule over every area of life—because when we function as we were designed, there is a divine power that changes everything. It renews and restores as the life of Christ is made manifest within our own. As we align ourselves under Him, there is an alignment that happens from deep within—where He brings about full restoration. It is an atmosphere that revives and makes whole.

As it impacts us, it impacts others—transforming every sphere of life in which we live. When each biblical sphere of life functions in accordance with God's Word, the outcomes are evangelism, discipleship, and community impact. As we learn how to govern ourselves under God, we then transform the institutions of family, church, and society from a biblically based kingdom perspective. Where through Him, we are touching heaven and changing earth.

To achieve our goal we use a variety of strategies, methods, and resources for reaching and equipping as many people as possible.

BROADCAST MEDIA

Hundreds of thousands of individuals experience *The Alternative with Dr. Tony Evans* through the daily radio broadcast playing on nearly one thousand radio outlets and in over 130 countries. The broadcast can also be seen on several television networks and is viewable online at TonyEvans.org.

LEADERSHIP TRAINING

The Kingdom Agenda Pastors (KAP) provides a *viable network* for *like-minded pastors* who embrace the Kingdom Agenda philosophy. Pastors have the opportunity to go deeper with Dr. Tony Evans as they are given greater biblical knowledge, practical applications, and resources to impact individuals, families, churches, and communities. KAP welcomes *senior and associate pastors* of all churches.

The Kingdom Agenda Pastors' Summit progressively develops church leaders to meet the demands of the twenty-first century while maintaining the Gospel message and the strategic position of the church. The Summit introduces *intensive seminars*, *workshops,* and *resources*, addressing issues affecting the community, family, leadership, organizational health, and more.

Pastors' Wives Ministry, founded by Dr. Lois Evans, provides *counsel*, *encouragement*, and *spiritual resources* for pastors' wives as they serve with their husbands in the ministry. A primary focus of the ministry is the KAP Summit that offers senior pastors' wives a safe place to *reflect, renew,* and *relax* along with training in personal development, spiritual growth, and care for their emotional and physical well-being.

COMMUNITY IMPACT

National Church Adopt-A-School Initiative (NCAASI) prepares churches across the country to impact communities by using *public schools as the primary vehicle for effecting positive social change* in urban youth and families. Leaders of churches, school districts, faith-based organizations, and other nonprofit organizations are equipped with the knowledge and tools to *forge partnerships* and build *strong social service delivery systems*. This training is based on the comprehensive church-based community impact strategy conducted by Oak Cliff Bible Fellowship. It addresses such areas as economic development, education, housing, health revitalization, family renewal, and racial reconciliation. We also assist churches in tailoring the model to meet the specific needs of their communities while simultaneously addressing the spiritual and moral frame of reference.

RESOURCE DEVELOPMENT

We are fostering lifelong learning partnerships with the people we serve by providing a variety of published materials. We offer booklets, Bible studies, books, CDs, and DVDs to strengthen people in their walk with God and ministry to others.

* * *

For more information, a catalog of Dr. Tony Evans'
ministry resources, and a complimentary copy of
Dr. Evans' devotional newsletter,
call (800) 800-3222,
or write TUA at P.O. Box 4000, Dallas TX 75208,
or log on to
TonyEvans.org.

NOTES

1. World Health Organization, "Global Health Observatory: HIV/AIDS," www.who.int/gho/hiv/en/.

2. See Romans 8:28.

3. George Bancroft, *History of the United States from the Discovery of the American Continent* (Boston: Little, Brown, and Company, 1875), 228–29. Google eBook.

4. See Romans 1:18–27.

5. See Psalm 33:12.

6. See Genesis 9:6.

7. Alexia Cooper and Erica Smith, "Homicide Trends in the United States, 1980–2008," U.S. Department of Justice (November, 2011): 2.

8. See Matthew 16:27; Romans 14:12; Revelation 20:11–15; each emphasize God holding mankind individually responsible to Him.

9. See Genesis 1:26–28.

10. See Ephesians 5:23; Ephesians 6:1; 1 Corinthians 11:3.

11. See Proverbs 14:34.

12. See 1 Timothy 5:4.

13. See Revelation 13:17.

14. Martin Luther King, Jr, "I Have a Dream . . .", August 28, 1963. www.archives.gov/press/exhibits/dream-speech.pdf.

15. James Strong, *Strong's Expanded Exhaustive Concordance of the Bible* (Nashville: Thomas Nelson, 2009), s.v. "*shamar*."

The Life Under God Series

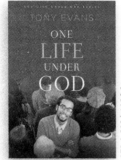

978-0-8024-1186-0

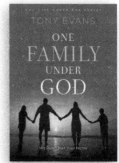

978-0-8024-1141-9

978-0-8024-1187-7

978-0-8024-1189-1

God's Word offers a biblically based kingdom agenda.
In The Life Under God series, Dr. Tony Evans highlights the four
areas which God has entrusted to us—personal, family, church,
and society—and demonstrates that Scripture has provided a clear
authority and a comprehensive approach to all of life.

MORE INFORMATION AVAILABLE AT THEKINGDOMAGENDABOOK.COM

MOODY
Publishers™

COMPLETE YOUR

DR. TONY EVANS

LIBRARY

IN THE KINGDOM AGENDA SERIES,

Dr. Tony Evans offers inexpensive resources which explore
God's intentions for life. Through masterful illustrations,
church members learn how to give sacrificially, thrive in
their marriages & activate the power of the cross.

MORE INFORMATION AVAILABLE AT THEKINGDOMAGENDABOOK.COM

MOODY
Publishers™

MORE INFORMATION AVAILABLE AT THEKINGDOMAGENDABOOK.COM

EVANS

THE URBAN ALTERNATIVE

At The Urban Alternative, the national ministry of Dr. Tony Evans, we seek to restore hope and transform lives to reflect the values of the kingdom of God. Along with our community outreach initiative, leadership training and family and personal growth emphasis, Dr. Evans continues to minister to people from the pulpit to the heart as the relevant expositor with the powerful voice. Lives are touched both locally and abroad through our daily radio broadcast, weekly television ministry and internet access points.

PRESENTING AN
ALTERNATIVE TO:

COMMUNITY OUTREACH

Equipping leaders to engage public schools and communities with mentoring, family support services and a commitment to a brighter tomorrow.

LEADERSHIP TRAINING

Offering an exclusive opportunity for pastors and their wives to receive discipleship from Drs. Tony and Lois Evans and the TUA staff, along with networking opportunities, resources and encouragement.

FAMILY AND PERSONAL GROWTH

Strengthening homes and deepening spiritual lives through helpful resources that encourage hope and health for the glory of God.

TONYEVANS.ORG

urbanpraise

Urban Praise, a commercial-free Moody Radio Internet station, offers a soulful blend of rich gospel and urban music. Energize your faith with artists like Kirk Franklin, Israel Houghton, Shirley Caesar, CeCe Winans, Walter Hawkins, and Lecrae, along with bite-size teaching segments from Tony Evans, Crawford Loritts, Melvin Banks, Beth Moore, and others.

www.urbanpraiseradio.org

MOODYRADIO

Where you turn. For life.

MOODYRADIO

Where you turn. For life.

Moody Radio produces and delivers compelling programs filled with biblical insights and creative expressions of faith that help you take the next step in your relationship with Christ.

You can hear Moody Radio on 36 stations and more than 1,500 radio outlets across the U.S. and Canada. Or listen on your smartphone with the Moody Radio app!

www.moodyradio.org